Conceptual Programming with Python

Thorsten Altenkirch   Isaac Triguero

© 2019 Thorsten & Isaac (Standard Copyright Licence)
ISBN 978-0-244-82276-7

Contents

1	Introduction		1
	1.1	Why Python?	1
	1.2	How to use Python?	3
	1.3	Where to find more information?	3
	1.4	Overview over the book	4
	1.5	About the authors	5
	1.6	Acknowledgments	6
2	Python from the top-level		9
	2.1	Basic types and operations	9
		2.1.1 Coercions	11
		2.1.2 Bool	13
		2.1.3 Functions	15
	2.2	Data structures	18
		2.2.1 Strings	18
		2.2.2 Lists	21
		2.2.3 Modifying lists	25
	2.3	Mysteries of Python	31
	2.4	Summary	33
	2.5	Solution to top-level challenge	35
	2.6	Quizzes	35
	2.7	Exercises	36
3	Imperative Programming		37
	3.1	Blocks of Code	37
	3.2	Inputs/Outputs	38
	3.3	Error handling	44
	3.4	Loops	45
		3.4.1 An example of the use of while loops	46
	3.5	The Halting problem	48
	3.6	Iterating through data structures	51

Contents

- 3.7 The guessing game 56
- 3.8 Summary 63
  - 3.8.1 Conditionals 63
  - 3.8.2 Handling Exceptions 65
  - 3.8.3 While loops 66
  - 3.8.4 For loops 67
- 3.9 Solution to Challenges 69
  - 3.9.1 Challenge 1 imperative programming .. 69
  - 3.9.2 Challenge 2 imperative programming .. 70
- 3.10 Quizzes 71
- 3.11 Exercises 72

4 Recursion and backtracking   75
- 4.1 Prelude: functions calling functions 75
- 4.2 The Tower of Hanoi 76
- 4.3 How is recursion executed? 82
- 4.4 Some combinatorics 86
  - 4.4.1 Factorial 86
  - 4.4.2 Binomial coefficents 88
- 4.5 Solving sudoku: Using backtracking 89
- 4.6 Summary 98
- 4.7 Solution to recursion challenge 98
- 4.8 Quizzes 101
- 4.9 Exercises 102

5 Object Oriented Programming   105
- 5.1 First example: a class for accounts 107
  - 5.1.1 Operations on objects 109
  - 5.1.2 Class variables 114
  - 5.1.3 Inheritance 117
  - 5.1.4 The __str__ method 120
- 5.2 Example: Implementing Expressions 123
  - 5.2.1 Printing expressions 129
  - 5.2.2 Evaluate expressions 131
- 5.3 Example: Creating a Knowledge Base 136
- 5.4 Summary 146
  - 5.4.1 Classes 146
  - 5.4.2 Objects 146

Contents

		5.4.3	Attributes (instance variables)	147
		5.4.4	Methods	147
		5.4.5	Class variables	147
		5.4.6	Inheritance	148
		5.4.7	Constructors (__init__)	148
		5.4.8	Print method (__str__)	149
		5.4.9	Data structures (trees)	149
	5.5	Solution to oop challenge		150
	5.6	Quizzes		153
	5.7	Exercises		153
6	**Functional Programming**			**159**
	6.1	Higher order functions and comprehension		160
	6.2	Laziness		164
	6.3	The sieve of Erathostenes		166
	6.4	Python in Python		168
	6.5	Challenge: if-then-else		174
	6.6	Summary		174
	6.7	Solution to the if-then-else challenge		175
	6.8	Quizzes		176
	6.9	Exercises		177
7	**Implementing games with pygame**			**179**
	7.1	What is Pygame?		180
		7.1.1	Installation and basics with pygame	181
	7.2	The Pong Game		185
		7.2.1	The Ball class	188
		7.2.2	The Paddle class	197
		7.2.3	Adding Lives and Score display	205
		7.2.4	Adding Sounds	208
		7.2.5	Adjusting the speed of the ball	208
	7.3	Project		212
8	**Getting started with Data Science**			**215**
	8.1	Data analysis with the Pandas library		215
	8.2	Visualising your data		228
	8.3	Mining the data		231
		8.3.1	A regression approach	231

v

Contents

		8.3.2	A classification approach	239
8.4	Summary			245
8.5	Solutions to Challenges			247
		8.5.1	Challenge 1	247
		8.5.2	Challenge 2	247
		8.5.3	Challenge 3	248
8.6	Exercises			251

1 Introduction

This book is based on a course for Master's Students at the School of Computer Science of the University of Nottingham. The course and the book are intended for students with little or no background in programming coming from different backgrounds educationally as well as culturally.

It is not mainly a Python course, but we use Python as a vehicle to teach basic programming concepts. Hence, the words *conceptual programming* in the title. The concepts covered are:

- data structures and a visual understanding of their representation on a computer,
- control structures in imperative programming,
- the Halting problem showing the limits of computability,
- the use of recursion to design algorithms,
- backtracking to solve hard problems,
- the basics of object oriented programming,
- the use of trees to represent structured data,
- concepts of functional programming,
- how to write an interpreter,
- basic software engineering via a game development project,
- the basics of data science.

This includes some material which we do not cover in our lectures due to lack of time.

1.1 Why Python?

Python is a modern language which is named after *Monty Python* the British comedians, not the snake. We are using Python for the course and this book for the following reasons:

1 Introduction

- Python has a very simple syntax with very little overhead. It uses layout to represent structure which is very natural and easy to read.
- Python uses dynamic typing, this makes it easy to learn because you don't have to get your head around a static type system, but see below.
- Python allows you to use concepts from a variety of programming paradigms, including object oriented programming and functional programming.
- There are a number of tools which make Python easy to use, like *jupyter notebooks* which we are using.
- Python features a *toplevel* like many functional languages, which makes it easy to interactively explore the language.
- Python is very popular, which results in a number of libraries (APIs) available in Python, which often makes it the language of choice in practice.

But it is hardly perfect. Here are some issues we have experienced with Python and which may make it a good idea to also look for other languages:

- The fact that Python doesn't use static typing means that many errors which would be flagged by other languages go undetected and may cause hidden errors in the software. This also means that interfaces are not clearly defined making the development of large systems harder.
- Python makes it often hard to use modern concepts, like recursion, because you have to pay an unnecessary performance penalty.
- Python also lacks certain features, like a pattern matching and algebraic data types, making the representation often unnecessarily clumsy.
- The lack of types leads to certain design errors in Python, for example the decision to avoid characters and represent them as strings.

However, weighing the reasons in favour and against we found that Python is the best choice for a course for beginners.

Our emphasis on concepts is important: you should be able to use them in any language you use for developing software.

1.2 How to use Python?

First of all you need to install Python, however it may already be installed since it is becoming a standard language. We are using the current version of Python which is Python 3.x ($x \geq 4$). We are using the Anaconda distribution which comes with a number of useful tools, but any other implementations should work fine too. However, we recommend using a version of Python that supports the use of a toplevel, which is not the case for some development environments.

Using Anaconda there are a number of ways to interact with Python:

- using the toplevel. This isn't specific to Anaconda, you just type `python` on your terminal and talk to the Python interpreter.
- using jupyter notebooks. That is a nice way to combine software development, exploration and documentation. Indeed, this book was written this way.
- using an integrated development environments (IDE) like *spyder* which comes with Anaconda, or *idle* which is part of the standard distribution.

1.3 Where to find more information?

There is so much material available on the internet now, that the students often get overwhelmed and confused. We have written this book to try to provide one consistent source of information for a course and suggest not to listen to too many chefs at the same time. That may spoil the soup.

On the other hand, we have tried to keep the material light, and we do not provide a complete reference manual to everything you may need. We recommend the following sources for additional information:

3

1 Introduction

- The Python Tutorial[1] is an excellent source of information.
- If you really want to know the details of some aspect of the language, check out the Python Reference manual[2], but be warned this is like reading a law book to find out about a legal problem.
- Often the standard library is more important than the language itself: check out the Library reference manual[3].
- For specific projects you need to consult the API documentation. For example for working with *pygame* you should consult the Pygame docs[4].
- Finally, no programmer can survive without Stackoverflow[5] any more, a rich repository of questions and answers and you can join and ask your own questions (and add your own answers). But be warned you can get very confused and spend a lot of time looking through stackoverflow conversations which in the end turn out to be irrelevant for your issue.

1.4 Overview over the book

We start with an exploration of Python from the top-level (Chapter 2), which covers some basic concepts like data types, coercions, functions and so on. We also introduce a graphical view of data structures in Python. Next we look at imperative programming (Chapter 3) which is the traditional way of programming present in Fortran or C. We introduce basic control structures like if-then-else and loops. We also discuss Turing's famous *Halting problem*. After this, we introduce one of the most powerful spells the young software wizard should master: recursion (Chapter 4), that is a function that calls itself. We are also using this to implement a sudoku solver via back-

---

[1] https://docs.python.org/3.6/tutorial/index.html
[2] https://docs.python.org/3.6/reference/
[3] https://docs.python.org/3.6/library/index.html
[4] http://www.pygame.org/docs/
[5] https://stackoverflow.com

tracking. Obviously, we cover Object Oriented Programming (Chapter 5) which is now a standard approach to program development. We also explain the use of *trees* to represent expressions and knowledge bases. An alternative to Object Oriented Programming is Functional Programming (Chapter 6), which is close to a mathematical understanding of programming. We also cover infinite data structures and how to write a Python interpreter in a functional style. Now you need to develop a bigger program, ideally in a group, and we suggest writing a game because it is fun and it is easy to understand what the goal is, hence we introduce the pygame library (Chapter 7). Finally, we give an introduction to Data Science which underlies the modern approach to Machine Learning (Chapter 8).

We present some *challenges* during the text, which you should try to solve yourself, but our solution is provided at the end of the chapter. Each chapter finishes with a quiz and exercises. The quiz can be easily done by using the Python interpreter but the point is to see whether you understand the language well enough to execute programs in your head. Indeed, the ability to run programs in your head is essential if you want to be able to write programs. The exercises are of different degrees of difficulty.

1.5 About the authors

Thorsten Altenkirch (also known as `Der Chef`) and Isaac Triguero (also known as `El Jefe`) are with the School of Computer Science of the University of Nottingham.

Thorsten is from Berlin, Germany and has grown up on the western side of the wall. Indeed it is a little known fact that the wall was only built for him and it was taken down 6 weeks after he left to start his PhD in Edinburgh, Scotland. Having worked as a programmer in Berlin for various companies, Thorsten got sucked into more theoretical realms doing a PhD on Type Theory which is a synthesis of logical reasoning and functional programming. Following this ambition he has been working in Gothenburg, Sweden and even in (for a Prussian

1 Introduction

from Berlin) more exotic places like Munich in catholic Bavaria. Eventually at the turn of the Millennium, Thorsten joined the School for Computer Science at the University of Nottingham where he founded the *Functional Programming Laboratory* together with his colleague Graham Hutton (check out Graham's Haskell book!). He ended up teaching Python after a sabbatical at the Institute for Advanced Study in Princeton which left him no other choice after his return. However, he has been enjoying teaching this course, especially since he was joined by his colleague Isaac.

Isaac was born and bred in a small town, called Atarfe, in the region of the magnificent Granada, Spain, where the emblematic Arabic palace and fortress 'Alhambra' sits. Unfortunately, he can't tell the Alhambra was built for him -- and luckily it was not demolished after his departure --, but he can undoubtedly say that it is way more beautiful than that Wall from Germany. Isaac studied his MSc and PhD degrees in Computer Science at the University of Granada, where he was drawn into all the buzz words of the moment (Data science and Big data) before departing to Ghent where he worked (and mostly ate waffles on a daily basis) as a postdoctoral researcher. A few years ago, Isaac joined the School of Computer Science at the University of Nottingham, and he was soon severely punished and trapped into teaching this programming course with the inimitable Thorsten. As a "junior" professor, working with the old and wise `Der Chef` and his bold teaching style has been a real challenge for him, but it turned to be a very rewarding experience, in which they ended up teaching each other quite a few things.

Thorsten and Isaac have mostly written this book together, but they led different chapters; you are challenged to guess who wrote what...

1.6 Acknowledgments

We would like to thank the students who have attended our course in the previous years and have provided a lot of feed-

1.6 Acknowledgments

back and useful suggestions which turned the course into what it is now. Their enthusiasm and the progress they were making motivated us to write this book. We would also like to thank the lab assistants who helped us with running the course and who also suggested many important improvements. We would like to thank Mikel Galar for reviewing the book and providing useful feedback. We thank Emilio Romero for creating the cover and Juan Triguero for drawing the pictures of us.

2 Python from the top-level

We can explore Python interactively by using the top level. This means we can type in Python code and Python will answer directly. Python has inherited this concept from functional programming languages like LISP or Haskell.

2.1 Basic types and operations

We can use Python as a calculator.

```
In : 3+5

Out: 8
```

Here we exploit the top-level built into *jupyter* which allows us to interactively evaluate Python programs. After `In:` you see what we have written, and after `Out:` you see Python's response.

We also have variables.

```
In : x=3

In : x+5

Out: 8
```

Did you notice? There is no `Out:` after the x=3? That is because Python doesn't produce any output after an assignment.

As usual in programming the '=' sign has a different meaning than in Mathematics. Here it means that we want to store something in a variable, which I draw as a shoebox which has a label on it.

2 Python from the top-level

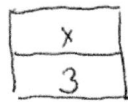

Unlike in many other programming languages we don't have to declare variables before using them. But they have to be initialised before we use them - otherwise we get an error.

```
In : x+y
```

```
-------------------------------------------------
NameError Traceback (most recent call last)
<ipython-input-4-259706549f3d> in <module>()  ---> 1x+y
NameError:  name 'y' is not defined
```

Instead of `Out:` we see an error message. Error messages can be confusing: first we see a *Traceback* telling us where the error occurred during execution (pretty obvious in this case) and then the type of error (here a *NameError*) and the error message.

We also have floating point numbers:

```
In : 3/4
```

```
Out: 0.75
```

And there are strings for text:

```
In : "Thor"
```

```
Out: 'Thor'
```

One can use either single '..' or double ".." quotes but the toplevel prefers to use '..' it seems. Sure, we can store strings in variables too.

```
In : me='Thor'
```

```
In : me
```

```
Out: 'Thor'
```

2.1 Basic types and operations

Data objects have types. We can use the function `type` to find out what type they are.

```
In : type(3+4)
```
```
Out: int
```

`int` stands for integer.

```
In : type(3/4)
```
```
Out: float
```

`float` is a floating point number.

```
In : type(me)
```
```
Out: str
```

and `str` is a string.

Note that it is not the variable `me` that has the type `str` but the object which is stored in it. We can also reuse `me` and store an integer.

```
In : me=42
```
```
In : type(me)
```
```
Out: int
```

This is called *dynamic typing*, because all the types in a program are determined when you run the code. The alternative is *static typing* where all the variables and operations have a fixed type which is known before you run your program. Static typing has the advantage that it avoids many errors but for beginners, dynamic typing is easier to understand.

2.1.1 Coercions

The operation + also works for strings. It means concatenation.

```
In : me+'sten'
```

2 Python from the top-level

```
TypeError                                 Traceback (most recent call last)
<ipython-input-15-6d2bddc8ae7e> in <module>()  ---> 1me+'sten'
TypeError:  unsupported operand type(s) for +:  'int' and 'str'
```

Oops, I forgot that I reused me. You see how error prone dynamic typing is - because this sort of error may occur when you run your program! Let's fix that.

```
In  :  me='Thor'
In  :  me+'sten'
Out:  'Thorsten'
```

Ok. I inadvertently also demonstrated that we cannot mix numbers and strings when using +.

```
In  :  me+3
```

```
TypeError                                 Traceback (most recent call last)
<ipython-input-18-391876a55bc2> in <module>()  ---> 1me+3
TypeError:  Can't convert 'int' object to str implicitly
```

We can convert data objects between different data types. For example we can convert a number to a string:

```
In  :  str(3)
Out:  '3'
In  :  me+str(3)
Out:  'Thor3'
```

We can also go the other way if we have a string that contains a number.

```
In  :  int('5')
Out:  5
```

These operations are called *coercions*. Python usually requires explicit coercions, while many other languages use implicit coercions (that is, they happen automatically). I prefer the Python approach while it is more verbose it is less error prone.

12

2.1 Basic types and operations

2.1.2 Bool

Another useful type is `bool` the type of booleans, or truth values.

```
In : type(True)

Out: bool

In : type(False)

Out: bool
```

We can also use logical operations on booleans

```
In : True and False

Out: False

In : True or False

Out: True

In : not True

Out: False
```

We can also use & for and and | for 'or'. But be wary they behave slightly different.

```
In : True & False

Out: False

In : True | False

Out: True
```

Some operations return booleans, for example the test for equality ==. You see this is very different from =.

```
In : x == 3

Out: True

In : x == "3"
```

13

2 Python from the top-level

```
Out: False
```

And we can combine the test with logical operations.

```
In : (x == 3) or (x == "3")

Out: True

In : (x == 3) and (str(x) == "3")

Out: True

In : type(x) == int

Out: True
```

You ask what is the difference between and and & for example? Ok here it is:

```
In : x=0

In : not (x==0) and 1/x==0

Out: False

In : not(x==0) & 1/x==0
```

```
----------------------------------------------
ZeroDivisionError Traceback (most recent call last)
<ipython-input-25-9bf9e76be849> in <module>() ---> 1not(x==0) &
1/x==0
    ZeroDivisionError: division by zero
```

In the first case Python decided that it didn't need to evaluate the 2nd part because false and anything is false. In the 2nd version it did evaluate the 2nd part which led to an error because we tried to divide by 0.

By the way, a shorthand for not (x==0) is x!=0.

14

2.1 Basic types and operations

2.1.3 Functions

The basic idea of a function is that it is a box where you can put something in and you get something out. We have functions in Python.

Let's define a function that adds 3 to its input and returns the result.

```
In : def f(x) :
         return x+3

In : f(2)

Out: 5
```

We are using a *parameter* in the definition of the function, I called it x. The *argument* of the function, e.g. 2 is assigned to the parameter x before the function is run. That is, there is a hidden assignment x = 2 which happens before the body of the function is executed. The parameter x only exists while the function is executed, it is not visible from outside.

Did you notice the : and the indentation? The : indicates that we start a new *block* of code which has to be indented. Later we will see that we can nest blocks which means we have to indent further. The combination of : and indentation replaces the use of { and } you see in many C-like languages. We will say more about this in the next section.

We use the keyword `return` to indicate what the function *returns*. We will soon see that there are also Python functions that don't return anything.

Here is another function that doubles its input:

```
In : def g(x) :
         return x+x

In : g(2)

Out: 4
```

We can combine both functions in calculations.

```
In : f(g(2))
```

15

2 Python from the top-level

```
Out: 7

In : g(f(2))

Out: 10
```

Did you notice when we say `f(g(2))` we run **first** `g` and then `f` even though we write first `f` and then `g`. This is the curse of Mathematics. We should really write something like $((2)g)f$ but it is too late to change that.

There is a type of functions:

```
In : type(f)

Out: function
```

Since Python doesn't have static types it doesn't have more specific type for functions either. A function can take any input and produce some output.

We can have functions working on strings too.

```
In : def talk(who,what) :
         return who+" is "+what

In : talk("Thor","stupid")

Out: 'Thor is stupid'
```

At the same time `talk` is also an example for a function that takes more than one parameter. No surprises here, I hope. We can use any number of parameters.

Let's define a function `isEven` which returns `True` if the input is an even integer and `False` otherwise.

We need to use the modulo operation % which calculates the remainder of a division. E.g.

```
In : 14%4

Out: 2
```

Because 14 divided by 4 is 3 remainder 2.

A number is even if the remainder from the division by 2 is 0.

2.1 Basic types and operations

```
In : 3%2

Out: 1

In : 4%2

Out: 0
```

Hence, we can define `isEven` as follows.

```
In : def isEven(n) :
         return n%2 == 0

In : isEven(5)

Out: False

In : isEven(8)

Out: True
```

Does this function satisfy our specification?

```
In : isEven("Thor")
------------------------------------------------------
  TypeError Traceback (most recent call last)
  <ipython-input-55-b02fb287e1a6> in <module>() --->
1 isEven("Thor")
    <ipython-input-52-77d3f3007053> in isEven(n)   1 def isEven(n) :
---> 2return n%2 == 0
  TypeError:  not all arguments converted during string
formatting
```

No :-(. We didn't say that it only works for integers but that it should return `True` if the input is an even integer and `False` otherwise.

Can we fix it?

```
In : def isEven(n) :
         return type(n) == int and n%2 == 0

In : isEven("Thor")

Out: False
```

17

2 Python from the top-level

```
In  : isEven(3)

Out: False

In  : isEven(4)

Out: True
```

What would happen if we had used & here instead of and? Can you figure it out in your head without actually running the code? This is an important skill if you want to become a good programmer!

Usually you won't define functions on the top-level but keep them in a file and edit them there. However, for the purposes of this book we will continue to show functions in the notebook.

2.2 Data structures

We have seen data types like integers, floats and booleans. A data structure is a data type which can be used to store other data in it. Actually the first example are strings which we have already seen.

2.2.1 Strings

We have already seen strings and the operation + to concatenate strings. Now, we look at some operations to access strings.

```
In  : s = "Thorsten"

In  : s[3]

Out: 'r'
```

s[n] returns the n+1th character - this is called indexing. Note that we are counting from 0 as we always do in computer science.

```
In  : s[0]

Out: 'T'
```

2.2 Data structures

There is no special type for characters but `s[n]` returns a string (of length 1).

```
In : type(s[3])
```

```
Out: str
```

Apropos length, there is a built-in function `len` that works on strings.

```
In : len(s)
```

```
Out: 8
```

Getting the last character of a string (which has index `len(s)-1` since we start counting at 0)

```
In : s[len(s)-1]
```

```
Out: 'n'
```

There is a shortcut for this:

```
In : s[-1]
```

```
Out: 'n'
```

```
In : s[-2]
```

```
Out: 'e'
```

This is quite particular to Python - this trick won't work in most other languages.

Instead of just one character we can also extract a part of a string. This is called *slicing*.

```
In : s[2:5]
```

```
Out: 'ors'
```

Note that this starts at index 2 (i.e. the 3rd character) and ends at index 4 (i.e the 5th character); that is one before 5.

What happens if the 2nd index is before the first?

2 Python from the top-level

```
In : s[5:2]

Out: ''
```

If we leave out the first index we start at the beginning:

```
In : s[:5]

Out: 'Thors'
```

If we leave out the last index we go until the end:

```
In : s[2:]

Out: 'orsten'
```

And if we leave out both? Exactly!

```
In : s[:]

Out: 'Thorsten'
```

This seems pretty useless at the moment but we will see...
Now a little challenge, construct a new string from s with the first and last characters swapped.

```
In : s[-1]+s[1:-1]+s[0]

Out: 'nhorsteT'
```

Has anything happened to s ?

```
In : s

Out: 'Thorsten'
```

Obviously not. Evaluating expressions doesn't change variables. In this respect, strings behave like numbers.
Can we turn this into a function?

```
In : def swap(x) :
        return x[-1]+x[1:-1]+x[0]
```

Let's test it.

20

2.2 Data structures

```
In : swap(s)

Out: 'nhorsteT'

In : swap("Python")

Out: 'nythoP'
```

What happens if we use *swap* twice?

```
In : swap(swap(s))

Out: 'Thorsten'
```

swap doesn't work for the empty string:

```
In : swap("")

IndexError Traceback (most recent call last)
<ipython-input-24-5b5714bf0d6e> in <module>() ---> 1swap("")
<ipython-input-20-46b07c57f25c> in swap(x) 1 def swap(x) :
---> 2return x[-1]+x[1:-1]+x[0]
IndexError: string index out of range
```

We get an error if we access a string beyond its length. In the case of the empty string the index 0 is already out of range.

But what happens to a string containing only one character?

```
In : swap("a")

Out: 'aa'
```

Question: Why did this happen? Can you figure it out?

2.2.2 Lists

Lists are like strings but they are sequences of anything while strings are sequences of characters. For example a sequence of numbers.

```
In : ns = [1,2,3]

In : type(ns)
```

2 Python from the top-level

```
Out: list
```

The items in a list can have different types, and in particular a list can contain lists again.

```
In : mixed = [1,"abc",[2,3,4]]
```

We can also coerce from and to lists, e.g.

```
In : list(s)
Out: ['T', 'h', 'o', 'r', 's', 't', 'e', 'n']
In : str(ns)
Out: '[1, 2, 3]'
```

Coercing into a string always produces the string that you see when you print the object.

All the operations we have seen on strings also work on lists.

```
In : ns+ns
Out: [1, 2, 3, 1, 2, 3]
In : ns+mixed
Out: [1, 2, 3, 1, 'abc', [2, 3, 4]]
In : ns[1]
Out: 2
In : mixed[2]
Out: [2, 3, 4]
In : mixed[1:3]
Out: ['abc', [2, 3, 4]]
In : mixed[2][2]
Out: 4
```

2.2 Data structures

The last example shows that we can repeat indexing operations (e.g. mixed[2] provides a list, so, mixed[2][2] is accessing the 3rd component of the list provided in mixed[2]). We can actually apply indexing to something else than a variable. Indeed, we can even write:

```
In : "Thor"[1]

Out: 'h'
```

This is useful when we want to represent a 2-dimensional structure, e.g. a matrix.

```
In : mat = [[1,2,3],[4,5,6],[7,8,9]]
```

Or maybe a better layout is:

```
In : mat =
     [[1,2,3],
      [4,5,6],
      [7,8,9]]

In : mat[1][2]

Out: 6
```

Do you remember the function `swap` we have defined earlier? Does it work for lists as well?

```
In : swap(ns)
     ----------------------------------------
     TypeError Traceback (most recent call last)
     <ipython-input-37-8cb49238f8fa> in <module>() ---> 1swap(ns)
     <ipython-input-20-46b07c57f25c> in swap(x)  1 def swap(x) :
     ---> 2return x[-1]+x[1:-1]+x[0]
       TypeError:  unsupported operand type(s) for +: 'int' and
     'list'
```

The problem is that the component of a list is usually not a list. In this case l[-1] is a number and we cannot + numbers and lists.

We can define a special version of swap for lists. We can turn an element into a list by putting [..] around it. E.g.

2 Python from the top-level

```
In : ns[-1]

Out: 3

In : [ns[-1]]

Out: [3]
```

We can use this to swap a list:

```
In : [ns[-1]]+ns[1:-1]+[ns[0]]

Out: [3, 2, 1]
```

Let's turn this into a function:

```
In : def swapl(xs) :
        return [xs[-1]]+xs[1:-1]+[xs[0]]

In : swapl(ns)

Out: [3, 2, 1]

In : swapl(list(s))

Out: ['n', 'h', 'o', 'r', 's', 't', 'e', 'T']
```

But this operation doesn't work for strings.

```
In : swapl(s)

-------------------------------------------------
TypeError Traceback (most recent call last)
<ipython-input-48-8daeb6f87815> in <module>()  ---> 1swapl(s)
<ipython-input-41-ebb51c35ddb6> in swapl(xs)   1 def swapl(xs) :
---> 2return [xs[-1]]+xs[1:-1]+[xs[0]]
TypeError:  can only concatenate list (not "str") to list
```

Challenge #1: Can we fix this? Can we define one function that works both for strings and for lists? (Section 2.5)

2.2 Data structures

2.2.3 Modifying lists

We can change lists. For example given my favourite list

```
In : ns = [1,2,3]
```

Let's say I want to change the 1st element (that is index 1) to 99. Here we go:

```
In : ns[0] = 99

In : ns

Out: [99, 2, 3]
```

That was easy. We can view a list as consisting of little boxes that can be changed individually just like the labelled boxes which correspond to variables. That is before the assignment we would draw the following image:

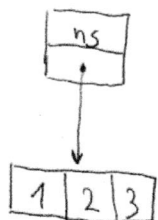

and after it looks like this:

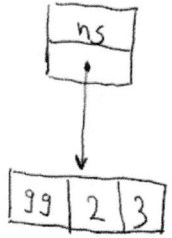

25

2 Python from the top-level

Before we have seen that the same operations worked for strings and for lists. If you now think that the update operation will also work for strings you will be disappointed:

```
In : me="Thor"

In : me[1]="x"
```

```
TypeError Traceback (most recent call last)
<ipython-input-7-dd2ce9adf30b> in <module>() ---> 1me[1]="x"
TypeError: 'str' object does not support item assignment
```

To make this visible I write a string directly into the variable box (the same as for numbers):

We say that strings are *immutable*, unlike lists which are *mutable*.

You may wonder why, especially since other programming languages do allow you to update strings. One reason is that knowing that you don't update strings can make the code more efficient because you can reuse a string as many times as you like.

However, we can always turn a string into a list first:

```
In : meList = list(me)

In : meList

Out: ['T', 'h', 'o', 'r']

In : meList[1] = "x"

In : meList

Out: ['T', 'x', 'o', 'r']
```

26

2.2 Data structures

Ok let's do the swap operation we have seen previously but this time we are going to modify a list.

First of all we restore the list (this is the problem with *destructive* operations).

```
In : meList = list(me)
```

Ok we are going to swap the first and the last element of the list, i.e. the items at index 0 and −1.

```
In : meList[0]=meList[-1]

In : meList[-1]=meList[0]
```

Let's see whether this has worked.

```
In : meList

Out: ['r', 'h', 'o', 'r']
```

Oops! This is not what I had in mind.
What has happened? Let's see, first restore the list (again).

```
In : meList = list(me)
```

Then do the first step.

```
In : meList[0]=meList[-1]

In : meList

Out: ['r', 'h', 'o', 'r']
```

Ok, now it is clear. When we did the 1st update we lost the original first character. Hence we have to save it before we change it.

Ok, let's start again.

```
In : meList = list(me)
```

We first store the first character:

```
In : helper = meList[0]
```

27

2 Python from the top-level

Then we copy the last character to the front.

```
In : meList[0] = meList[-1]

In : meList

Out: ['r', 'h', 'o', 'r']
```

And now we set the last character to the saved first character.

```
In : meList[-1] = helper
```

And voila!

```
In : meList

Out: ['r', 'h', 'o', 'T']
```

We can put this into a function. I call it `swapx` where the x stands for change.

```
In : def swapx(lst) :
         helper = lst[0]
         lst[0] = lst[-1]
         lst[-1] = helper
```

`swapx` is our first example of a function that doesn't return anything but it just does something.

We can use this to restore meList.

```
In : meList

Out: ['r', 'h', 'o', 'T']

In : swapx(meList)

In : meList

Out: ['T', 'h', 'o', 'r']
```

What is the difference between the function `swapl` and `swapx`? Both work on lists.

`swapl` returns a list but doesn't change the list.

```
In : meList
```

2.2 Data structures

```
Out: ['T', 'h', 'o', 'r']

In : swapl(meList)

Out: ['r', 'h', 'o', 'T']

In : meList

Out: ['T', 'h', 'o', 'r']
```

While `swapx` doesn't return anything but changes the data structure.

```
In : meList

Out: ['T', 'h', 'o', 'r']

In : swapx(meList)

In : meList

Out: ['r', 'h', 'o', 'T']
```

While swapx is called a *function* in Python, it isn't really a mathematical function. It changes the memory of the computer, it modifies boxes. E.g. we can draw the memory before running `swapx`

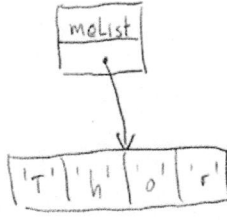

and after:

29

2 Python from the top-level

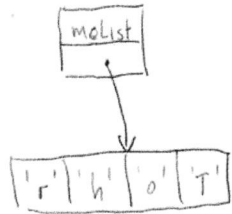

Ok, how do we swap twice? (Admittedly not a very useful operation).
For `swap1` it works like this.

```
In : meList = list(me)

In : swap1(swap1(meList))

Out: ['T', 'h', 'o', 'r']
```

And for `swapx`?

```
In : swapx(swapx(meList))
```

```
-----------------------------------------------------
TypeError Traceback (most recent call last)
<ipython-input-46-aa6bb992929e> in <module>() --->
1 swapx(swapx(meList))
<ipython-input-30-c5848f168542> in swapx(lst)   1 def swapx(lst)
:  ---> 2 helper = lst[0]   3 lst[0] = lst[-1]   4 lst[-1] = helper
TypeError:  'NoneType' object is not subscriptable
```

This is a strange error. What has happened?

As I said `swapx` doesn't return anything. Actually it returns `nothing`. And this is fed into the outer call of `swapx` which doesn't know what to do with it.

To do `swapx` twice we just have to run it twice. Like this:

```
In : meList = list(me)

In : meList

Out: ['T', 'h', 'o', 'r']
```

30

```
In : swapx(meList)
     swapx(meList)

In : meList

Out: ['T', 'h', 'o', 'r']
```

In Python there is actually a way to define swapx without using the helper variable. Python allows a parallel assignment, that is we can update both boxes in parallel:

```
In : def swapx(lst) :
        lst[0],lst[-1] = lst[-1],lst[0]
```

2.3 Mysteries of Python

Can we write a `swapx` function that works for strings?

Clearly, we cannot use the assignment operation to a component of a string. But on the top-level we can change a variable that contains a string. E.g.

```
In : me = "Thor"

In : me = swap(me)

In : me

Out: 'rhoT'
```

So what stops me from turning this into a function?

```
In : def swapsx(s) :
        s = swap(s)
```

Ok, let's test this.

```
In : me = "Thor"

In : swapsx(me)

In : me

Out: 'Thor'
```

31

2 Python from the top-level

This was not what we expected! No change!

What has happened? The variable `s` is a parameter, it is a box that only exists while we execute the function `swapsx`. When we call `swapsx(me)` we copy the *content* of `me` into `s`. So indeed at the end of the execution of `swapsx` the box `s` contains the swapped version of the string but nothing has happened to `me`.

There is no operation in Python (unlike e.g. in C) which creates a reference to a top-level variable - hence it is not possible to write a function that updates an arbitrary top-level variable. However, it is possible to update a specific top-level variable.

```
In : def swapme() :
         global me
         me = swap(me)

In : me

Out: 'Thor'

In : swapme()

In : me

Out: 'rhoT'
```

The declaration `global me` tells Python that `me` is a *global* variable and not a local one.

We have already seen that we can update lists in a function, which is because they are a data structure that contains boxes and we update those boxes and not the content of the variable box on the top-level.

But can we use the `swapl` function instead of doing the assignments? Clearly, if we just do the same as for strings it won't work. That is the following attempt:

```
In : def swaplx(lst) :
         lst = swapl(lst)
```

It doesn't work. But there is a clever way to make this work. It turns out that in Python we can also replace slices of lists. That is for example:

```
In : meList = list("Thor")

In : meList

Out: ['T', 'h', 'o', 'r']

In : meList[1:]="im"

In : meList

Out: ['T', 'i', 'm']
```

And hence using the apparently useless `lst[:]` we can change the whole list.

```
In : def swaplx(lst) :
         lst[:] = swapl(lst)

In : meList = list("Thor")

In : swaplx(meList)

In : meList

Out: ['r', 'h', 'o', 'T']
```

2.4 Summary

We can evaluate expressions or assign values to variables using x = e where e is some expression.

Basic types in Python :

- Integers (`int`)
- Floating point numbers (`float`)
- Strings (`str`)
- Truthvalues (`bool`)
- Functions (`function`)
- Lists (`list`)

Use `type(..)` to find out the type of an object. Use the name of a type as a function to coerce a value to that type, if possible.

2 Python from the top-level

Integers and Floats

We have the usual arithmetic operations like +, -, * and **
(exponentation). Note that / on integers produces a float while
// will produce an integer while % computes the remainder.

Strings and Lists

String constants can be written either "..." or '...'. Lists are
written as [a1 , a2 , ..].

+ is concatenation. You can access the nth element of a string
or a list using x[n], we start counting from 0. Using negative
numbers counts from the end where -1 is the last item. You can
slice using x[m:n]; this produces the substring/list starting at
m and ending at n-1. If you leave out the first index the default
is 0 and if you leave out the last the default is -1. len(x)
computes the length of a string or a list.

You can modify lists by using index or slice expressions on
the left hand side of an assignment. Strings cannot be modified.

Truthvalues

Basic truthvalues are True and False. We can combine truthvalues using and, or and not. Alternatively we can use & and
| which always evaluate all components.

Basic predicates return truthvalues such as == equality and
<,<=,> and >= which compare numbers and other data types.
!= is inequality.

Functions

Functions are defined starting with

```
def f (x1 , x2 , .. , xn) :
```

followed by an indented block of code. Here xi are the parameters of the function. The block may contain a statement
return e which means that the function returns the value

e. Variables in functions are local unless they are explicitly marked as global using

```
global x1,x2,..
```

2.5 Solution to top-level challenge

The challenge was to create a program that would perform the functional swap operation both for lists and for strings. The trick is to use slicing instead of indexing because it works the same for both lists and strings.

```
In : def swap (x) :
        return x[-1:]+x[1:-1]+x[:1]

In : swap(list("Thor"))

Out: ['r', 'h', 'o', 'T']

In : swap("Thor")

Out: 'rhoT'
```

2.6 Quizzes

```
In : myString = [["1","a"],0,[""]]
```

what is the output of each of the following lines. Try to figure this out in your head and on paper without using Python first - then you can check you answers using Python.

1. myString[0][0][0]
2. myString[myString[1]][0]+myString[2]
3. myString[0][1]+myString[2][0]
4. myString[0:1]+myString[1:2]
5. myString[int(myString[0][0])]

2 Python from the top-level

2.7 Exercises

1. Define a function rotateR with one argument (a string) that returns the string rotated to the right. E.g. `rotateR("Thor")` should return `"rTho"`.

2. Define a function rotateL with one argument (a list) that returns the list rotated to the left. E.g. rotateL([1,2,3,4]) should return [2, 3, 4, 1].

3. Do both functions work for lists and strings? If not, how can you fix that?

4. Define a function rotateRx that gets a list as a parameter and changes that list by rotating it to the right. The function should return nothing. E.g. we assign `l = [1,2,3,4]` and then run `rotateRx(l)` (which returns nothing). If we now check `l` it returns `[4, 1, 2, 3]`.

5. Can you modify 4. so that it works for strings?

6. Write a function `rotateR2` that gets a string as an argument and returns the string rotated to the left twice, using only the function `rotateR` from the 1st exercise. E.g. `rotateR2("Thor")` should return `'orTh'`.

7. Write a function `rotateRx2` that changes its parameter (a list) by rotating it twice to the right. The function should only use rotateRx from part 4. E.g. we assign `l = [1,2,3,4]` and then run `rotateRx2(l)` (which returns nothing). If we now check `l` it returns `[3, 4, 1, 2]`.

8. Can you create a list `l` that prints as `[[1, 2, 3], [1, 2, 3]]` but when I rotate only the first part by `rotateRx(l[1])` and then print l it turns out that both parts have been rotated, i.e. I get

   `[[3, 1, 2], [3, 1, 2]]`

3 Imperative Programming

What does Imperative programming mean? In the imperative programming[1] style, statements are executed in some order determined by the programmer.

- **Atomic statements** are assignments (e.g. x=3), input (e.g. input("What's your name")), output (e.g. print()).

- **Control structures** contain other statements and determine the flow of control.

- We can follow the flow of control by pointing at the part of the program which is executed next.

Examples of control structures are:

- **Conditionals**: if, elif, else
- **Loops**: while, for
- **Exception handling**: try except

3.1 Blocks of Code

Code is normally organised in a number of blocks that combine several statements.

- In C-like languages, we typically use { . . . } to do this. In those languages, the indentation only serves to improve readability.
- A good program layout reflects the nesting of blocks by indentation. We will see a few examples below.

---

[1] https://en.wikipedia.org/wiki/Imperative_programming

3 Imperative Programming

- In Python, we don't need curly braces { and } but the layout determines the program structure.
- A new block is indicated by colons : and an increased indentation of the statements belonging to the block.
- Usually indentation is increased by 4 characters (== a tab).

3.2 Inputs/Outputs

Inputs/Outputs refer to the communication of a user and a program. The simplest way for a program to output information is using the built-in `print` function that will print out the values of variables. This will be typically printed by default in the standard output (`std.stdout`), which means the screen. Let's start with the classical 'Hello World' message:

```
In : print("Hello World!")

Hello World!
```

We have seen before that there are functions that return a value, and functions that simply perform an operation and do not return anything. When we invoke the `print` function, it does not `return` anything. However, we get the text in the standard *output* (i.e. the screen) for the user.

If we check the type of the print function:

```
In : type(print)

Out: builtin_function_or_method
```

Python tells us that this is a built-in function, which means that this function belongs natively to Python.

What happens if we assign the output of a `print` statement to a variable?

```
In : output = print("hello")

hello
```

3.2 Inputs/Outputs

Interestingly, we did get the output printed as before. However, what is the content of the variable `output`?:

```
In : output
```

As you may have guessed, if we run the above cell, it will not return anything, could we try printing it?

```
In : print(output)

None
```

Python prints `None`, meaning that there is no content in the variable `output`. Actually, if we check the type of this variable, we will see that it doesn't have any:

```
In : type(output)

Out: NoneType
```

As input, we could ask the user to input a string, and save it in a variable:

```
In : name = input("What's your name? ")

What's your name? Isaac
```

If we now check the content of the variable `name`:

```
In : name

Out: 'Isaac'
```

So, we can use the function `input` to get an input from the user (from the keyboard), and it could be a string or an integer, but we need to be careful. For example, if we ask for the time:

```
In : time = input("What time is it? ")

What time is it? 1437
```

39

3 Imperative Programming

What is the type of time?

```
In : time

Out: '1437'

In : type(time)

Out: str
```

The `input` function will always return a string. Thus, if you want to get an integer, you need to coerce the output of the function `input`:

```
In : time = int(input("What's time is it? "))

What's time is it? 1200


In : time

Out: 1200
```

If we now check the type:

```
In : type(time)

Out: int
```

Task: Let's create a simple program that asks for your name and the time, and say Hi <name>, good morning/afternoon. How do we do this?

```
In : name = input("What's your name? ")
     time = int(input("What time is it? "))

     if time < 1200:
         print("Hi "+name + ", good morning!")
     else:
         print("Hi "+name + ", good afternoon!")

What's your name? Isaac
What time is it? 1443
Hi Isaac, good afternoon!
```

3.2 Inputs/Outputs

We have added a control structure, known as *if-else*, that changes the flow of the program depending on the content of the variable `time`. So, on the above program only one `print` statement will be run.

Note that with control structures such as *if-else*, indentation really matters. If you don't use the correct indentation or you forget the colons the program won't compile! Or it could run but print erroneously more outputs than you wanted to.

Let's see a more complete program that also says 'good evening':

```
In : name = input("What's your name? ")
     time = int(input("What time is it? "))

     if time < 1200:
         print("Hi "+name + ", good morning!")
     else:
         if time <1800:
             print("Hi "+name + ", good afternoon!")
         else:
             print("Hi "+name + ", good evening!")


What's your name? Isaac
What time is it? 1900
Hi Isaac, good evening!
```

In the above code, we have made use of nested blocks! The second *if-else* block is included within the `else` block of the first *if-else*. This means that the second block is only considered when `time >= 1200`.

This composed *if-else* structure consists of multiple lines of code, but it is effectively a single statement. Then, it goes to the next line. See the following "good bye" statement:

```
In : name = input("What's your name? ")
     time = int(input("What time is it? "))

     if time < 1200:
         print("Hi "+name + ", good morning!")
     else:
         if time <1800:
```

41

3 Imperative Programming

```
                print("Hi "+name + ", good afternoon!")
        else:
                print("Hi "+name + ", good evening!")

    print("Good Bye")

What's your name? Isaac
What time is it? 2000
Hi Isaac, good evening!
Good Bye
```

There are still a number of things I don't like from the previous code. For example, we could reduce the nesting of the multiple conditions by using `elif`:

```
In : name = input("What's your name? ")
    time = int(input("What time is it? "))

    if time < 1200:
        print("Hi "+name + ", good morning!")
    elif time <1800:
        print("Hi "+name + ", good afternoon!")
    else:
        print("Hi "+name + ", good evening!")

    print("Good bye")

What's your name? Isaac
What time is it? 0900
Hi Isaac, good morning!
Good bye
```

But also, we repeat the same 'Hi + name' three times... Can we make this nicer?

```
In : name = input("What's your name? ")
    time = int(input("What time is it? "))

    print("Hi "+ name)

    if time < 1200:
        print(", good morning!")
    elif time <1800:
        print(", good afternoon!")
```

3.2 Inputs/Outputs

```
    else:
        print(", good evening!")

    print("Good bye")
What's your name? Isaac
What time is it? 1200
Hi Isaac
, good afternoon!
Good bye
```

That worked! But it is not nice. It prints two lines!

Challenge #1: Investigate how to create a program that prints the output in a single line. Hint: Use the `help` in Python to know more about the `print` function (Section 3.9.1).

What happens if we input something 'silly' as the time?

```
In : name = input("What's your name? ")
     time = int(input("What time is it? "))

    print("Hi "+ name)

    if time < 1200:
        print(", good morning!")
    elif time <1800:
        print(", good afternoon!")
    else:
        print(", good evening!")

    print("Good bye")
What's your name? Isaac
What time is it? I don't know

    ---------------------------------------------
    ValueError Traceback (most recent call last)
    <ipython-input-1-eab9e61d1349> in <module>  1 name =
input("What's your name?  ") ---> 2time = int(input("What time
is it? "))  3  4 print("Hi "+name)  5
    ValueError: invalid literal for int() with base 10: "I don't
know"
```

Python errors are not 'nice' for the end-user of the program. How do we handle them?

43

3 Imperative Programming

3.3 Error handling

In Python, like in many other programming languages, there are specific control structures to handle exceptions. To do so, we will use try and except blocks. A `try` block code will be stopped and control is transferred down to the `except` block in case that an error is encountered.

Let's see this with one example:

```
In : name = input("What's your name? ")

    try:
        time = int(input("What time is it? "))
    except ValueError:
        print("This is not a number!")

    print("Hi "+name )

    if time < 1200:
        print(", good morning!")
    elif time <1800:
        print(", good afternoon!")
    else:
        print(", good evening!")

    print("Good bye")

What's your name? Isaac
What time is it? I don't really know
This is not a number!
Hi Isaac
```

```
    NameError Traceback (most recent call last)
.   <ipython-input-1-93751fb6804c> in <module>()  8 print("Hi
"+name )   9 ---> 10if time < 1200:    11 print(", good morning!")
12 elif time <1800:
    NameError:  name 'time' is not defined
```

You may get no error or a different error if on your system the variable `time` is already defined.

The code in the `try` block is executed but once an error occurs then the `except` block matching the error is executed. If the error doesn't match, then the program will crash as before. If the `try` block is executed successfully, the next statement after the `except` (they can be several for different errors) is executed.

However, we would like to give the user the opportunity to enter a correct input. We want to keep asking until the time is entered correctly.

3.4 Loops

To achieve this, we need to use a `while` loop which repeats a (nested) block of code until a logical condition becomes `False` (See more in Section 3.8.3). We end up with the following program:

```
In : done = False
     while not done :
         try:
             time = int(input("What time is it? "))
             done = True
         except ValueError:
             print("Incorrect input!")
What time is it? What
Incorrect input!
What time is it? Why?
Incorrect input!
What time is it? 1020
```

In this example we use a variable holding a boolean value, `done` (this is often called a *flag*). Initially, it is set to `False` (because we are not done) but once we successfully set the time, it is set to `True`. Accordingly, the loop terminates when the logical condition is checked the next time (after the body has been executed).

Alternatively, we can avoid the use of a flag and instead exit the loop via a `break` statement. The logical condition now doesn't play a role, and we just use `True` which means the loop is executed forever unless terminated explicitly for example via a `break`.

3 Imperative Programming

```
In : while True :
         try:
             time = int(input("What time is it? "))
             break
         except ValueError:
             print("Incorrect input!")
What time is it? shut
Incorrect input!
What time is it? up
Incorrect input!
What time is it? 1500
```

Another statement we can use in a loop is `continue` which means that we jump to the end of the body of that block, that is, the condition is checked and if true the body is executed again. We will see a use of this soon.

3.4.1 An example of the use of while loops

A common use of `while` loops is to check an arithmetical condition. As an example, we use this to implement Euclid's algorithm which calculates the greatest common divisor of two integers: that is the greatest number that divides both inputs without remainder. This can be achieved from subtracting the smaller from the larger number until they are equal.

We implement this as a function:

```
In : def gcd (x , y):
         while x != y :
             if x < y :
                 y = y - x
             else :
                 x = x - y
         return x
```

Here are some tests:

```
In : gcd(26,18)

Out: 2

In : gcd(49,70)
```

3.4 Loops

```
Out: 7
```

It is worthwhile to run the algorithm by hand a few times, keeping track of the changing variable values and the position of execution in the program.
Will the program always terminate?

```
In : gcd(2,0)
```
```
KeyboardInterrupt Traceback (most recent call last)
<ipython-input-15-d9ff8bd8e19b> in <module>()  ---> 1gcd(2,0)
<ipython-input-8-4d2c5b793de8> in gcd(x, y)   1 def gcd (x , y):
---> 2while x != y :    3 if x < y :    4 y = y - x  5 else :
KeyboardInterrupt:
```

No, in this case the loop was running forever. The only way out was to interrupt the computation (e.g. by pressing Control-C).

In the case of `gcd` it is quite easy to see for which inputs the function will terminate. However, this is not always so easy. Here is a famous sequence[2] which was invented by a Mathematician called Collatz. It works like this:

- You start with any positive integer and then
  - you divide it by 2 if it is even,
  - you multiply it by 3 and add 1 otherwise.
- We stop when we reach the number 1.

We implement a function which prints the Collatz sequence starting with a given number.

```
In : def collatz(n) :
        while n != 1 :
            print(n,end = ",")
            if n % 2 == 0 :
                n = n // 2
            else :
                n = 3 * n + 1
        print(1)
```

---

[2]https://en.wikipedia.org/wiki/Collatz_conjecture

47

3 Imperative Programming

Let's try some cases:

```
In : collatz(7)

7,22,11,34,17,52,26,13,40,20,10,5,16,8,4,2,1

In : collatz(27)

27,82,41,124,62,31,94,47,142,71,214,107,322,161,484,242
,121,364,182,91,274,137,412,206,103,310,155,466,233,700
,350,175,526,263,790,395,1186,593,1780,890,445,1336,668
,334,167,502,251,754,377,1132,566,283,850,425,1276,638,
319,958,479,1438,719,2158,1079,3238,1619,4858,2429,7288
,3644,1822,911,2734,1367,4102,2051,6154,3077,9232,4616,
2308,1154,577,1732,866,433,1300,650,325,976,488,244,122
,61,184,92,46,23,70,35,106,53,160,80,40,20,10,5,16,8,4,
2,1

In : collatz(97)

97,292,146,73,220,110,55,166,83,250,125,376,188,94,47,1
42,71,214,107,322,161,484,242,121,364,182,91,274,137,41
2,206,103,310,155,466,233,700,350,175,526,263,790,395,1
186,593,1780,890,445,1336,668,334,167,502,251,754,377,1
132,566,283,850,425,1276,638,319,958,479,1438,719,2158,
1079,3238,1619,4858,2429,7288,3644,1822,911,2734,1367,4
102,2051,6154,3077,9232,4616,2308,1154,577,1732,866,433
,1300,650,325,976,488,244,122,61,184,92,46,23,70,35,106
,53,160,80,40,20,10,5,16,8,4,2,1
```

This sequence is also called the roller-coaster sequence... The question is: does the sequence always terminate?, that is, does it always end with 1? It turns out that nobody knows the answer, it is an open problem to either show that the Collatz sequence always terminates or to find an example for which it doesn't.

3.5 The Halting problem

In general, it is hard to see whether a program with while loops will ever stop, we say *terminate*. Actually this problem is famously called the *halting problem* and it is a prime example

3.5 The Halting problem

which can be specified precisely but it cannot be solved by a computer. This was first observed by the British Mathematician Alan Turing[3], and he published a paper showing that there is no program that can solve the Halting problem[4] in 1936, so actually just before the first computers were built.

To prove his result, Turing developed the concept of a Turing machine[5] which is an imaginary computing device consisting of an infinite tape and a control unit. However, to understand the argument we don't need to study Turing machines, we can just use Python instead.

Okay, let's assume something, and then we show that it leads to a logical inconsistency. This way we know that our assumption is false. Our assumption is that there is a Python function

```
def halts(fun,arg) :
    ...
```

which gets two string arguments: `fun` which contains a function definition and `arg` which is an argument and the function will return `true` if the Python program which we get when applying `fun` to the argument terminates and `false` otherwise.

We need to make the specification a bit more precise: the string may contain invalid Python code or it may throw an exception when run in all these cases the function returns `false`. Also, we don't want the result to depend on any input (or the state of some files) hence it should also return `false` if any input is attempted.

Now we can use the function `halts` to define another function:

```
def weird(fun) :
    def halts(fun,arg) :
        ...
    if halts(fun,fun) :
        while(true) :
```

---

[3]https://en.wikipedia.org/wiki/Alan_Turing
[4]https://en.wikipedia.org/wiki/Halting_problem
[5]https://en.wikipedia.org/wiki/Turing_machine

3 Imperative Programming

```
        pass
   else :
        return
```

`weird` gets a string as argument that may contain Python code. It contains the code for `halts` (yes we can define functions inside another function) and it uses `halts` to determine whether this function applied to its own code will terminate. If it does, `weird` goes into an infinite loop and otherwise it just returns.

Now let's define a variable `wstr` that contains the code for `weird` as a string, i.e. we define

```
wstr =
"""
def weird(fun) :
 ...
"""
```

Now what happens if we run

```
weird(wstr)
```

Weird! If `weird` applied to its own code would terminate then `halts(wstr,wstr)` will return `true` and hence `weird(wstr)` will not terminate. If on the other hand `weird(wstr)` will not terminate then `halts(wstr,wstr)` will return `false` and hence `weird(wstr)` will terminate.

Okay, this is a logical impossibility: `weird(wstr)` will terminate exactly when it will not terminate. This shows that our assumption is impossible: There is no Python program that computes `halts`. And since we can write interpreters for one programming laguage in another, the problem is the same for any programming language, including Turing machines.

We say that the Halting problem is *undecidable*. There are actually many undecidable problems, for example it is undecidable whether a logical formula in predicate logic (using operations with variables like $\forall$ (forall) and $\exists$ (exists)) is true. One can show that if one could decide all logical formulas then one could also decide the Halting problem, and we have just seen that this is impossible.

3.6 Iterating through data structures

We have been working with different data structures (e.g. lists) before, and we learned how to index/slice them. But, how can we access the different elements of a list automatically?

We could define a function `sum`, for example, to compute the sum of a list of integers.

```
In : lst = [1,2,3]

In : def sum (lst) :
         s = 0
         while lst != [] :
             s += lst[0]
             lst = lst[1:]
         return s

In : sum(lst)

Out: 6
```

The above solution works well, but it is not very elegant, and it requires to modify the list step by step. Since it is a common problem to *iterate* over a data structure (e.g. a list) there is a special construct for it.

To do so, we will use a different iterative control structure, known as `for`:

```
In : def sum (lst) :
         s = 0
         for i in lst :
             s += i
         return s
```

With a `for` structure, the variable `i` will iteratively be assigned with the values in `lst` (one by one).

```
In : sum(lst)
```

3 Imperative Programming

```
Out: 6
```

We can also use this to print a table of numbers and their squares.

```
In : print("n \t| n**2")
     for i in [1,2,3,4,5] :
         print("{} \t| {}".format(i,i**2))

n       | n**2
1       | 1
2       | 4
3       | 9
4       | 16
5       | 25
```

(The "\t" means tab, go to the next tabulator position).

It would get very laborious to create increasing lists of numbers by hand, hence there is a function for this (range).

```
In : print("n \t| n**2")
     for i in range(1,5):
         print("{} \t| {}".format(i,i**2))

n       | n^2
1       | 1
2       | 4
3       | 9
4       | 16
```

Let's check what range is doing!

```
In : range(1,5)

Out: range(1, 5)

In : type(range(1,5))

Out: range
```

Weird, isn't it? Probably you were not expecting that. range produces an object which for can iterate over but which is not visible. However, we can coerce it to a list.

3.6 Iterating through data structures

```
In : list(range(1,5))

Out: [1, 2, 3, 4]
```

So, `range` provides a list of number from the number specified as the first argument to the number specified in the last argument minus one.

We can vary the parameters of range:

- If you do not specify a range, it will assume [0, number - 1]

```
In : list(range(5))

Out: [0, 1, 2, 3, 4]
```

- You can also modify the increment (e.g. two by two)

```
In : list(range(1,10,2))

Out: [1, 3, 5, 7, 9]
```

- This could also be a decrement!

```
In : list(range(10,1,-2))

Out: [10, 8, 6, 4, 2]
```

We can combine `sum` and `range`, e.g. compute the sum of the numbers from 1 to 100

```
In : sum(range(1,101))

Out: 5050
```

There is a famous story that this can be computed by a simple formula which the famous German Mathematician Gauss discovered when he was in school and was given the task to calculate the sum of the numbers 1 to 100. Gauss realised that the pairwise addition of terms from opposite ends of the list yielded identical intermediate sums: $1 + 100 = 101$, $2 + 99 = 101$, $3 + 98 = 101$, and so on, for a total sum of $50 \times 101 = 5050$.

We can thus implement this method as:

53

3 Imperative Programming

```
In : def gauss(n) :
         return n*(n+1)//2

In : gauss(100)

Out: 5050
```

Let's now implement a function that reverses a list:

```
In : def rev(lst) :
         tsl = []
         for x in lst :
             tsl = [x] + tsl
         return tsl

In : rev([1,2,3])

Out: [3, 2, 1]
```

We could also use *for-loops* to print truth tables:

```
In : booleans = [False, True]

In : print("x \t not x")
     for x in booleans :
         print("{} \t {}".format(x, not x))

x          not x
False      True
True       False
```

For and and or we need nested loops

```
In : print("{} \t| {}\t|{}|{} | {}"\
           .format("x","y","x and y","x or y","x == y"))
     for x in booleans :
         for y in booleans :
             print("{} \t| {}\t| {}\t| {}\t| {}"\
                   .format(x,y,x and y,x or y,x==y))

x       | y      |x and y|x or y | x == y
False   | False  | False | False | True
False   | True   | False | True  | False
True    | False  | False | True  | False
True    | True   | True  | True  | True
```

54

3.6 Iterating through data structures

We are constructing a truth table for one of the *de Morgan laws*: this one says that negating an **and** is the same as the **or** of its negated components, that is `not (x and y)` is always the same as `(not x) or (not y)`. E.g. saying *it is not the case that the sun shines and the dog barks* is logically equivalent to saying *the sun doesn't shine or the dog doesn't bark*. Think about it.

```
In : print("{} \t| {}\t| {}\t| {}   | {}". \
           format("x","y","not(x and y)", \
                  "(not x) ", ".. == .."))
      print("\t|\t|\t\t| or (not y) |\t")
      for x in booleans :
          for y in booleans :
              print("{} \t| {}\t| {}\t\t| {}\t     | {}" \
                    .format(x,y,not(x and y), \
                            (not x) or (not y), \
                            not(x and y) == (not x) \
                            or (not y)))
```

```
x       | y       | not(x and y)  | (not x)      | .. == ..
        |         |               | or (not y)   |
False   | False   | True          | True         | True
False   | True    | True          | True         | True
True    | False   | True          | True         | True
True    | True    | False         | False        | True
```

The equivalence is always true, this is called a tautology. We may first think that `not (x and y)` is the same as `(not x) and (not y)` but it is easy to see that this is a fallacy by constructing the truth table:

```
In : print("{} \t| {}\t| {}\t  | {}\t| {}". \
           format("x","y","not","(not x) ", \
                                   ".. == .."))
      print("\t|\t| (x and y)| and (not y)\t|")
      for x in booleans :
          for y in booleans :
              print("{} \t| {}\t| {}\t  | {}\t| {}". \
                    format(x,y,not(x and y), \
                           (not x) and (not y), \
                           not(x and y) == (not x) \
                           and (not y)))
```

55

3 Imperative Programming

```
x       | y       | not     | (not x)        | .. == ..
        |         | (x and y)| and (not y)   |
False   | False   | True    | True           | True
False   | True    | True    | False          | False
True    | False   | True    | False          | False
True    | True    | False   | False          | False
```

This one is not a tautology. We can define a function corresponding to each formula.

```
In : def dm(b,c) :
         return not(b and c)== (not b) or (not c)

In : dm(True,False)

Out: True

In : def dmx(b,c) :
         return not(b and c)== (not b) and (not c)

In : dmx(False,True)

Out: False
```

Challenge #2: Can you write a tautology checker that determines whether a given function on two variables is a tautology? (Section 3.9.2)

E.g. it should work as follows:

```
isTauto(dm) = True

isTauto(dmx) = False
```

3.7 The guessing game

As an exercise to play around with imperative programming, we implement **the guessing game**. This consists of asking the user to guess a number that the computer has randomly chosen. The computer will keep on asking the user for their input

56

3.7 The guessing game

until he/she guesses it correctly. The program should handle wrong inputs from the user.

So, the first thing that we need for this program is that the computer thinks of a (random) number. To do this, we will make use of a random number generator. We need to import the library `random` which is built-in in Python:

```
In : import random
```

We can check how `random` works by using the built-in help: `help(random)`. It has a function `randint` that provides a random number within a range [a,b]:

```
In : random.randint(0,100)

Out: 56
```

There are many more libraries in Python, and we will introduce them when we need them. Note that we have to prefix all the calls to functions within the random library with `random`. We could have avoided this but this could create name clashes (i.e. our code and the library or different libraries use the same name), hence we will not do this here.

So, our program could start by storing this random number in a variable and printing a message saying that it is thinking of a number:

```
In : secret = random.randint(0,100)
     print("I am thinking of a number...")

I am thinking of a number...
```

I am going to print the `secret` to test the program as we write it.

```
In : print(secret)
```

30

3 Imperative Programming

Then, the program will continuously ask the user for his/her guess until they have guessed it correctly. We could simply use a while loop that will break only when the user introduces the right number. Remember that the input will be a number, so we have to coerce the input.

```
In : while True:
         guess = int(input("What is your guess? "))

         if guess == secret :
             print("That's right!")
             break

What is your guess? 65
What is your guess? 30
That's right!
```

The game would be too difficult if the program does not give you a *hint* if the number is higher or lower than the number you tried. So, we are going to add conditions to tell the user if their guess is lower or higher than the `secret` number:

```
In : while True:
         guess = int(input("What is your guess? "))

         if guess == secret :
             print("That's right!")
             break
         else:
             if guess < secret:
                 print ("My number is bigger")
             else:
                 print ("My number is smaller")

What is your guess? 65
My number is smaller
What is your guess? 50
My number is smaller
What is your guess? 30
That's right!
```

As we did before, we could refactor the if-else structure by using `elif` and avoid nesting!

3.7 The guessing game

```
In : while True:
        guess = int(input("What is your guess? "))

        if guess == secret :
            print("That's right!")
            break
        elif guess < secret:
            print ("My number is bigger")
        else:
            print ("My number is smaller")
```

What happens if the user does not introduce a number?

```
In : while True:
        guess = int(input("What is your guess? "))

        if guess == secret :
            print("That's right!")
            break
        elif guess < secret:
            print ("My number is bigger")
        else:
            print ("My number is smaller")

What is your guess? I don't know
```

```
-----------------------------------------------
ValueError Traceback (most recent call last)
<ipython-input-19-e070fd1bf9a0> in <module>  1 while True:
---> 2guess = int(input("What is your guess? "))  3  4 if guess
== secret :    5 print("That's right!")
ValueError:  invalid literal for int() with base 10:   "I don't
know"
```

As before, we encounter an error, which should be handled appropriately using `try` and `except`!

```
In : while True:
        try:
            guess = int(input("What is your guess? "))
        except ValueError :
            # incorrect format, report and ask again.
            print("Please input a number")
            continue
```

59

3 Imperative Programming

```
        if guess == secret :
            print("That's right!")
            break
        elif guess < secret:
            print ("My number is bigger")
        else:
            print ("My number is smaller")
```

```
What is your guess? I dont know
Please input a number
What is your guess? 28
That's right!
```

We have used `continue` to skip the code below if an error is triggered. Thus, when the user does not introduce a number, we will continue running from the beginning of the while loop, asking again for their guess.

It could also happen that the user does introduce a number, but it happens to be a very big number; To keep the game simple, the number should be between a range [`minguess`,`maxguess`]; if the given number is below `minguess` or above `maxguess`, we should print a message asking the user to introduce a different number within that range. Once again, we use `continue` to skip the lines below and ask again for a new guess.

```
In : while True:
        try:
            guess = int(input("What is your guess? "))
        except ValueError :
            # incorrect format, report and ask again.
            print("Please input a number")
            continue

        if guess < 1 or guess > 100 :
            print("Please input a number between {} and {}"\
                .format(1,100))
            continue

        if guess == secret :
            print("That's right!")
            break
        elif guess < secret:
```

3.7 The guessing game

```
            print ("My number is bigger")
        else:
            print ("My number is smaller")
What is your guess? 900
Please input a number between 1 and 100
What is your guess? 30
That's right!
```

In the above program, we have 'hard'-coded the minimum and maximum values for the guess. This is a bad practice in programming, because if we now want to change the program to work on a different range (e.g. [-10,10]), we need to change the values in multiple parts of our program (first when the program chooses a random number and then to check the range and print the message). To avoid this, we could use two variables at the beginning of the code to store `minguess` and `maxguess`.

```
In :  import random

    minguess = 1
    maxguess = 100

    secret = random.randint(minguess,maxguess)
    print("I am thinking of a number...")

    while True:
        try:
            guess = int(input("What is your guess? "))
        except ValueError :
            # incorrect format, report and ask again.
            print("Please input a number")
            continue

        if guess < minguess or guess > maxguess :
            print("Please input a number between {} and {}"\
                .format(minguess,maxguess))
            continue

        if guess == secret :
            print("That's right!")
            break
        elif guess < secret:
```

3 Imperative Programming

```
            print ("My number is bigger")
        else:
            print ("My number is smaller")
```

```
I am thinking of a number...
What is your guess? 50
My number is bigger
What is your guess? 75
My number is smaller
What is your guess? 62
My number is bigger
What is your guess? 68
My number is smaller
What is your guess? 64
My number is bigger
What is your guess? 66
That's right!
```

In the above code, we have used a very clever way to output the values of minguess and maxguess. We have used the function format to format a string. This could have been done concatenating the variables with the text and using coercion. However, the format function simplifies this!

```
In : print("Please input a number between " + str(minguess) \
        + " and " + str(maxguess))

Please input a number between 1 and 100
```

To improve the program we would also like to count the number of guesses that the user has introduced! We will use a variable count that is initialised to 0, but we need to be careful when to increment the value of count (not to account for errors introducing a number).

```
In : import random

    minguess = 1
    maxguess = 100

    secret = random.randint(minguess,maxguess)
    print("I am thinking of a number...")
```

3.8 Summary

```
    count = 0 # number of guesses

    while True :
        try :
            guess = int(input("What is your guess? "))
        except ValueError :
            # incorrect format, report and ask again.
            print("Please input a number")
            continue
        # we are checking the range
        if guess < minguess or guess > maxguess :
            print("Please input a number between {} and {}"\
                  .format(minguess,maxguess))
            continue
        count += 1
        if guess == secret :
            print("That's right!")
            break
        elif guess < secret :
            print("My number is bigger")
        else :
            print("My number is smaller")
    print("You needed {} guesses.".format(count))

I am thinking of a number...
What is your guess? 50
My number is smaller
What is your guess? 25
My number is smaller
What is your guess? 12
My number is smaller
What is your guess? 6
My number is bigger
What is your guess? 9
That's right!
You needed 5 guesses.
```

3.8 Summary

3.8.1 Conditionals

```
In : name="Isaac"
     time=1000
     if time < 1200 :
```

3 Imperative Programming

```
        print("Good morning "+ name)
    elif time < 1800 :
        print("Good afternoon "+name)
    else :
        print("Good evening "+name)
Good morning Isaac
```

- Code is executed depending on the boolean conditions.
- We can use:
    - Just `if`.
    - `if` with `else`.
    - `if` followed by an arbitrary number of `elif` and finished with `else`
- `elif` is shorthand for `else` and `if` but avoids too much nesting of blocks.

A few examples of conditional blocks:

```
In : condition1 = condition2 = True

    if condition1:
        if condition2:
            print("condition1 AND condition2 are True")
condition1 AND condition2 are True
```

Wrong indentation:

```
In : if condition1:
        if condition2:
        print("condition1 AND condition2 are True")
  File "<ipython-input-5-dab58914b6ed>", line 4 print("condition1
AND condition2 are True") # This line is wrongly indented ^
IndentationError: expected an indented block
```

```
In : condition1 = True

    if condition1:
        print("This will be printed if condition1 is True")

        print("This print statement is within the if-block")
```

3.8 Summary

```
This will be printed if condition1 is True
This print statement is within the if-block
```

```
In : if condition1:
        print("This will be printed if condition1 is True")

    print("This print statement is outsite the if-block")

This will be printed if condition1 is True
This print statement is outsite the if-block
```

```
In : if condition1:
        print("This will be printed if condition1 is True!")
    else:
        print("This will be printed if condition1 is False!")

This will be printed if condition1 is True!
```

```
In : if condition1:
        print("This will be printed if condition1 is True!")
    else:
        if condition2:
            print("This will be printed if condition1 is \
            False and condition2 is True!")
        else:
            print("This will be printed if both condition1\
            and condition2 are False!")

This will be printed if condition1 is True!
```

An alternative way to write the previous code with less nesting:

```
In : if condition1:
        print("This will be printed if condition1 is True!")
    elif condition2:
        print("This will be printed if condition1 is False \
        and condition2 is True!")
    else:
        print("This will be printed if both condition1 and \
        condition2 are False!")

This will be printed if condition1 is True!
```

3 Imperative Programming

3.8.2 Handling Exceptions

```
In : try:
         time = int(input("What is the time?"))
     except ValueError:
         print("Please input an integer!")

What is the time?what?
Please input an integer!
```

- We can catch runtime errors and execute some handling code when it occurs.
- If an error occurs during the execution of the block after try, it is checked whether the error is caught in except in which case the block after except is executed.
- `ValueErrors` are generated by failed coercions. There are many other errors.

Question: will the following code ever trigger an exception?

```
In : try:
         time = input("What is the time?")
     except ValueError:
         print("Please input an integer!")

What is the time?xxx
```

As the `input` function will always provide a string, it does not matter the input the user introduces that this will never trigger an exception. In this case, we don't need to use try-except!

3.8.3 While loops

While loops repeat a block of code (i.e. indented code below the while) until the condition is `False`.

- The condition is checked, if true the block is executed and this is repeated until the condition is false.
- Within a loop, we can use the special statements:

3.8 Summary

- **break**: the loop is terminated and the next statement after the loop is executed.
- **continue**: we continue immediately with checking the condition etc.

* Frequently we use loops with while True that run forever until they are terminated by a break. You can also use flags instead.

```
In : # Collatz
     n=10
     while n > 1 :
         print(n, end=", ")
         if n % 2 == 0:
             n = n // 2
         else:
             n = 3*n + 1
     print(1)
10, 5, 16, 8, 4, 2, 1
```

3.8.4 For loops

* For loops allow us to iterate over the elements of a data structure (lists, sets, strings).
* Each time the variable gets assigned the next element of the data structure and the loop terminates when there are no further elements left.
* To implement simple counting loops we use the range function.

```
In : for i in range(1,10) :
         print(i)
1
2
3
4
5
6
7
8
9
```

67

3 Imperative Programming

Note that `range(1,10)` does not include the 10!

```
In : list(range(10))

Out: [0, 1, 2, 3, 4, 5, 6, 7, 8, 9]
```

We needed to coerce this to a list, otherwise range doesn't show you a list!

```
In : list(range(2,7))

Out: [2, 3, 4, 5, 6]

In : list(range(1,9,2))

Out: [1, 3, 5, 7]

In : list(range(9,-1,-1))

Out: [9, 8, 7, 6, 5, 4, 3, 2, 1, 0]
```

You can read more about the `range` function by using in-line help: `help(range)`.

With for loops, we are not limited to lists of integers, we can iterate through strings for example:

```
In : for word in ["scientific", "computing", "with", "Python"]:
         print(word)

scientific
computing
with
Python

In : for letter in "Isaac":
         print(letter)

I
s
a
a
c
```

Note that we can also use `break` and `continue` in for-loops.

3.9 Solution to Challenges

```
In : total   = 0
    for element in range(1000):
        if element > 100:
            break     # This breaks the for loop
        total += element

    total, element

Out: (5050, 101)
```

In the following example, `continue` will jump to the for loop again without printing the elements.

```
In : total = 0
    for element in range(20):
        if element % 2 != 0:
            continue
        print(element)
        total += element
    total

0
2
4
6
8
10
12
14
16
18

Out: 90
```

3.9 Solution to Challenges

3.9.1 Challenge 1 imperative programming

Investigate how to create a program that prints the output in a single line. Hint: Use the `help` in Python to know more about the `print` function.

If we look at the documentation of the `print` function, you will see that we need an additional parameter:

69

3 Imperative Programming

```
In : name = input("What's your name? ")
    time = int(input("What time is it? "))

    print("Hi "+name, end="")

    if time < 1200:
        print(", good morning!")
    elif time <1800:
        print(", good afternoon!")
    else:
        print(", good evening!")

    print("Good bye")
What's your name? Isaac
What time is it? 1200
Hi Isaac, good afternoon!
Good bye
```

This code fixes the problem with the unnecessary line break. We added an optional, named parameter `end = ""` to `print`. The parameter defaults to `"\n"` which stands for newline. We can replace it by any other string, e.g.

```
In : print("ab", end=",")
    print("cd", end=".")
ab,cd.
```

3.9.2 Challenge 2 imperative programming

Can you write a tautology checker that determines whether a given function on two variables is a tautology? E.g. it should work as follows:

```
isTauto(dm) = True

isTauto(dmx) = False

In : def isTauto(f) :
        for x in [True,False] :
            for y in [True,False] :
                if not f(x,y) :
                    return False
        return True
```

3.10 Quizzes

isTauto uses two nested loops to test f for all possible inputs. If it ever returns false then isTauto will also return false. If however, we reach the end of the loop we know that f always returned true and we also retrun true.

```
In : isTauto(dm)

Out: True

In : isTauto(dmx)

Out: False
```

3.10 Quizzes

What is the output of each of the following Python programs?

```
In : b = True
    c = not b
    if b and c :
        print("a")
    elif b or c :
        print("b")
    else :
        print("c")

In : try :
        x = str(7)
        print("a")
    except ValueError:
        print("b")

In : b=True
    while b :
        print("a",end="")
        b = not b
        if b :
            break
        else :
            continue
        print("b",end="")
    print("c",end="")
```

71

3 Imperative Programming

```
In : try :
         x = int("x")
         print("7",end="")
     except ValueError :
         print("8")

In : x=[1]
     try :
         x = list(str(x))
         print(x,end="")
     except :
         print(x,end="")
```

3.11 Exercises

Exercise 01: You are asked to implement a Python program that plays the **number guessing game**. The user thinks of a number between 1 - 100 (but does not input anything to the program); Your program should ask questions to the user to know whether the number is less than, equal or greater than another number. The goal is to guess the answer with as few steps as possible.

Here is how a run of the program must look like:

```
Think of a number between 1 and 100!
Is your number greater (>), equal (=),
or less (<) than 50?
Please answer <,=, or >! >
Is your number greater (>), equal (=),
or less (<) than 75?
Please answer <,=, or >! <
Is your number greater (>), equal (=),
or less (<) than 62?
Please answer <,=, or >! <
Is your number greater (>), equal (=),
or less (<) than 56?
Please answer <,=, or >! >
Is your number greater (>), equal (=),
or less (<) than 59?
Please answer <,=, or >! >
Is your number greater (>), equal (=),
```

3.11 Exercises

```
or less (<) than 60?
Please answer <,=, or >! =
I have guessed it!
I needed 6 steps!
```

Please take the following points into consideration:

- Your program should handle incorrect inputs by printing an error message and asking the user to answer again.
- The program should require a minimal number of steps.
- The program should spot if the information the user provided is inconsistent (i.e. the user is lying).
- The program should behave exactly as in the example above, i.e. it should play the game only once and use the same interface.
- The code should be as simple as possible and easily understandable. Comments should be used where appropriate.
- It should be straightforward to modify the code to use a different interval, e.g. -10 and +10.

4 Recursion and backtracking

We are now moving to one of the biggest *magic* tricks of programming: *recursion*. By recursion we simply mean a function calling itself but does this actually make sense?

4.1 Prelude: functions calling functions

We have already seen functions. Functions are there to do a job and they can in turn use other functions. Just to make a very simple example: Let's say we are programming a robot and we implement a move function `move(f,t)` moves some object from a position called `f` to a position `t`. Ok, I am just going to fake it and print a line, like this:

```
In : def move(f,t) :
         print("Move object from {} to {}!".format(f,t))
```

Let's test it:

```
In : move("A","B")

Move object from A to B!
```

I am leaving the robot programming bit as an exercise. Now we want to implement another function which moves an object via an intermediate position, that is `moveVia(f,v,t)` moves the object first from `f` to `v` and then from `v` to `t`. My point is that we don't want to repeat all the sophisticated robot programming we have done when implementing `move` but instead we are using `move`:

4 Recursion and backtracking

```
In : def moveVia(f,v,t) :
        move(f,v)
        move(v,t)
```

A little test run:

```
In : moveVia("A","C","B")

Move object from A to C!
Move object from C to B!
```

Ok, this should be rather obvious. The point is that a function calls other functions to accomplish its task. Now does it ever make sense that a function calls itself? Like this one:

```
In : def foo(x):
        foo(x)
```

What happens if we run this function?

```
In : foo(4)

    ----------------------------------------------------
    RecursionError Traceback (most recent call last)
    <ipython-input-10-a9edc735bc6b> in <module> ---> 1 foo(4)
    <ipython-input-9-b13b35069de0> in foo(x)   1 def foo(x):   --->
    2 foo(x)
    ...  last 1 frames repeated, from the frame below ...
    <ipython-input-9-b13b35069de0> in foo(x)   1 def foo(x):   --->
    2 foo(x)
    RecursionError: maximum recursion depth exceeded
```

That doesn't look very useful! Let's look at a more useful application of recursion.

4.2 The Tower of Hanoi

We've got three rods, and a number disks (of different sizes).

4.2 The Tower of Hanoi

The puzzle starts with the disks in a neat stack in ascending order of size on one rod, the smallest at the top.

Goal: To shift all the disks from the first rod to the last rod. We need to comply with these rules:

- Only one disk can be moved at a time.
- Each move consists of taking the upper disk from one of the stacks and placing it on top of another stack or on an empty rod.
- No disk may be placed on top of a smaller disk.

At this point it is a good idea to play a bit around and try to solve the puzzle for a small number of disks. E.g. for 3 and then 4. If you don't have the toy just try it with pen and paper.

Our goal is now to write a Python function that solves the problem for any number of disks. That is, we are going to implement a function:

```
def hanoi(n,f,h,t)
```

where n is the number of disks, and f,h,t are the names we want to use for the from, the helper and the target rod, respectively (we will see that this flexibility will turn out to be quite useful).

4 Recursion and backtracking

So, for example

```
hanoi(4,"A","B","C")
```

should produce the instructions for how to solve the puzzle with 4 disks:

```
Move disk from A to B
Move disk from A to C
Move disk from B to C
Move disk from A to B
Move disk from C to A
Move disk from C to B
Move disk from A to B
Move disk from A to C
Move disk from B to C
Move disk from B to A
Move disk from C to A
Move disk from B to C
Move disk from A to B
Move disk from A to C
Move disk from B to C
```

The basic idea is that we can use the recipe for n disks to solve the problem for n+1 disks. To be more concrete, let's assume we know how to solve the puzzle for 3 disks and we want to figure out the solution for 4 disks.

That is in the beginning it looks like this:

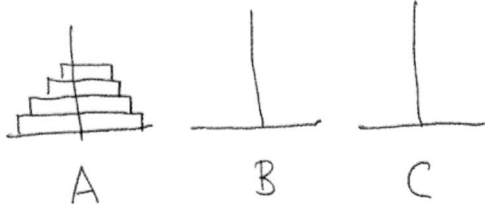

Now we use the fact that we know how to solve the problem for 3 disks to move 3 disks from A to B this time using C as the helper,

4.2 The Tower of Hanoi

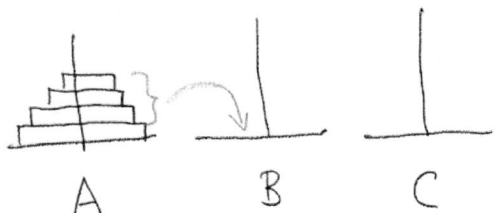

that is in Python we invoke

`hanoi(3,"A","C","B")`

After this it looks like this:

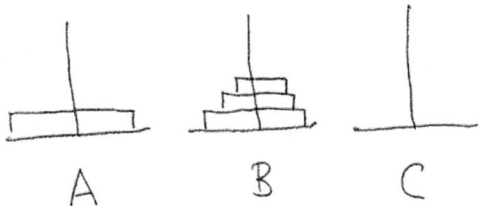

Next we move the big disk from A to C

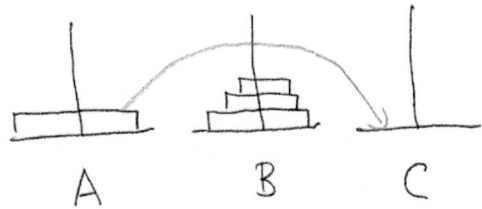

In Python we simply print a message to the user

`print("Move disk from {} to {}".format("A","C"))`

and the result is:

4 Recursion and backtracking

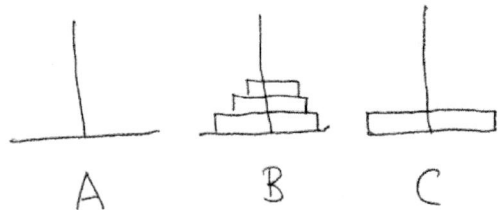

We are almost done but now we need to employ again the solution for 3 disks and move the 3 disks from B to C this time using A as the helper.

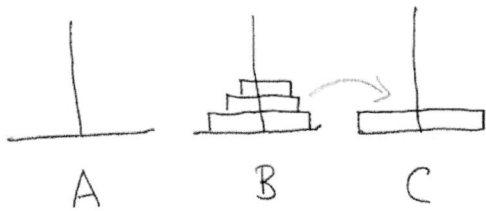

in Python we say

```
hanoi(3,"B","A","C")
```

and we end up with the intended placement:

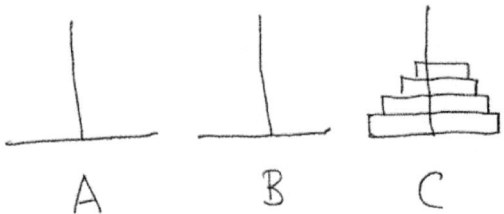

Clearly the choice of 4 and 3 and the specific names of rods was merely accidently and we can turn the whole idea into one generic Python function:

4.2 The Tower of Hanoi

```
In : def hanoi(n,f,h,t):
        hanoi(n-1,f,t,h)
        print("Move disk from {} to {}".format(f,t))
        hanoi(n-1,h,f,t)
```

However, this doesn't work yet. If we call it we get the same error as before.

```
In : hanoi(4,"A","B","C")
```

```
RecursionError Traceback (most recent call last)
<ipython-input-7-0d5272c34002> in <module> --->
1hanoi(4,"A","B","C")
  <ipython-input-6-34f928f5bdc0> in hanoi(n, f, h, t)   1 def
hanoi(n,f,h,t):   ---> 2hanoi(n-1,f,t,h)   3 print("Move disk from
{} to {}".format(f,t))   4 hanoi(n-1,h,f,t)
  ...   last 1 frames repeated, from the frame below ...
  <ipython-input-6-34f928f5bdc0> in hanoi(n, f, h, t)   1 def
hanoi(n,f,h,t):   ---> 2hanoi(n-1,f,t,h)   3 print("Move disk from
{} to {}".format(f,t))   4 hanoi(n-1,h,f,t)
RecursionError: maximum recursion depth exceeded
```

Clearly we have to stop at some point. Our program tried to move negative numbers of disks around before crashing.

We need to identify a *base case* which we can solve without recursion. What is the base case for this example?

You may think that the easiest case is the one where we have just one disk in which case we simply move it from the initial rod to the final one without using the helper.

However, there is an even easier case: the problem with 0 disks. In this case we have to do nothing. This leads to the following program:

```
In : def hanoi(n,f,h,t):
        if n==0:
            return
        else:
            hanoi(n-1,f,t,h)
            print("Move disk from {} to {}".format(f,t))
            hanoi(n-1,h,f,t)
```

And indeed this works!

```
In : hanoi(4,"A","B","C")
```

81

4 Recursion and backtracking

```
Move disk from A to B
Move disk from A to C
Move disk from B to C
Move disk from A to B
Move disk from C to A
Move disk from C to B
Move disk from A to B
Move disk from A to C
Move disk from B to C
Move disk from B to A
Move disk from C to A
Move disk from B to C
Move disk from A to B
Move disk from A to C
Move disk from B to C
```

4.3 How is recursion executed?

The solution to the tower of Hanoi problem seems to use a bit of magic. What is actually happening when a function calls itself? In particular what is happening with the local variables and the parameters?

When we call the function initially, as in `hanoi(4,"A","B","C")`, it is clear what the values of all the parameters are, that is n is 4, and f,h,t are "A","B" and "C", respectively. But then when `hanoi` calls itself invoking `hanoi(3,f,t,h)` the first time n is 3 and f is "A" (as before) but h and t are "C" and "B", that is, they have switched. Moreover, once this call is finished the old values are restored and when we execute `print("Move disk from {} to {}".format(f,t))` we actually print `Move disk from A to C` using the old values of the parameters.

We can actually convince ourselves that this is what happens by 'instrumenting' our program, so that, it prints out the values of the parameters each time it is called. To make it readable, I indent it by the recursion depth which is just 4-n, assuming for simplicity that we are only interested in the case fo 4 disks.

```
In : def hanoi(n,f,h,t):
        print("{}n={},f={},h={},t={}"\
```

82

4.3 How is recursion executed?

```
            .format(" "*(4-n),n,f,h,t))
      if n==0:
          return
      else:
          hanoi(n-1,f,t,h)
          print("{}Move disk from {} to {}"\
                .format(" "*(4-n),f,t))
          hanoi(n-1,h,f,t)

In : hanoi(4,"A","B","C")
n=4,f=A,h=B,t=C
 n=3,f=A,h=C,t=B
  n=2,f=A,h=B,t=C
   n=1,f=A,h=C,t=B
    n=0,f=A,h=B,t=C
    Move disk from A to B
    n=0,f=C,h=A,t=B
   Move disk from A to C
   n=1,f=B,h=A,t=C
    n=0,f=B,h=C,t=A
    Move disk from B to C
    n=0,f=A,h=B,t=C
  Move disk from A to B
  n=2,f=C,h=A,t=B
   n=1,f=C,h=B,t=A
    n=0,f=C,h=A,t=B
    Move disk from C to A
    n=0,f=B,h=C,t=A
   Move disk from C to B
   n=1,f=A,h=C,t=B
    n=0,f=A,h=B,t=C
   Move disk from A to B
   n=0,f=C,h=A,t=B
 Move disk from A to C
 n=3,f=B,h=A,t=C
  n=2,f=B,h=C,t=A
   n=1,f=B,h=A,t=C
    n=0,f=B,h=C,t=A
   Move disk from B to C
   n=0,f=A,h=B,t=C
  Move disk from B to A
  n=1,f=C,h=B,t=A
   n=0,f=C,h=A,t=B
  Move disk from C to A
   n=0,f=B,h=C,t=A
 Move disk from B to C
 n=2,f=A,h=B,t=C
```

4 Recursion and backtracking

```
n=1,f=A,h=C,t=B
n=0,f=A,h=B,t=C
Move disk from A to B
n=0,f=C,h=A,t=B
Move disk from A to C
n=1,f=B,h=A,t=C
n=0,f=B,h=C,t=A
Move disk from B to C
n=0,f=A,h=B,t=C
```

Ok, we can see that this works correctly but how is it done actually? The main ingredient is the 'stack' that is a part of the computer memory which is used in a 'last-in-first-out' fashion, that is what is put in last is taken out first. Each time a function is called the current values of the parameters and the local variables are put onto the stack and when the function returns the old values are restored from the stack.

That is in our example after we call `hanoi(4,"A","B","C")` we are in the following situation:

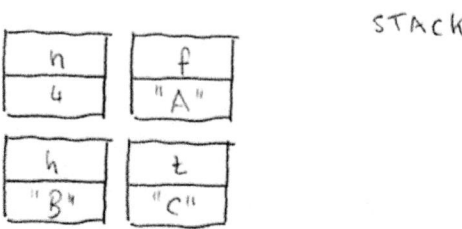

Here the stack is empty (actually it would already contain some information but we ignore that). We are growing the stack downwards. Then after we call `hanoi(3,f,t,h)` it looks like this

4.3 How is recursion executed?

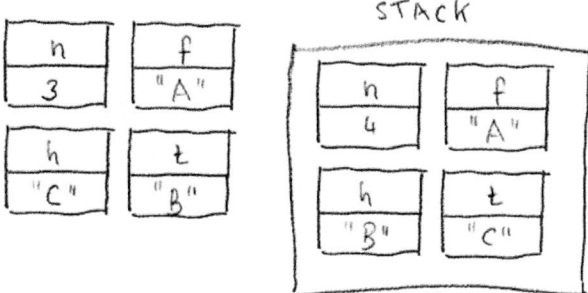

We have saved the old values of the parameters on the stack and have assigned the new value. Within hanoi(3,f,t,h) we call hanoi(2,f,h,t) which results in the following picture:

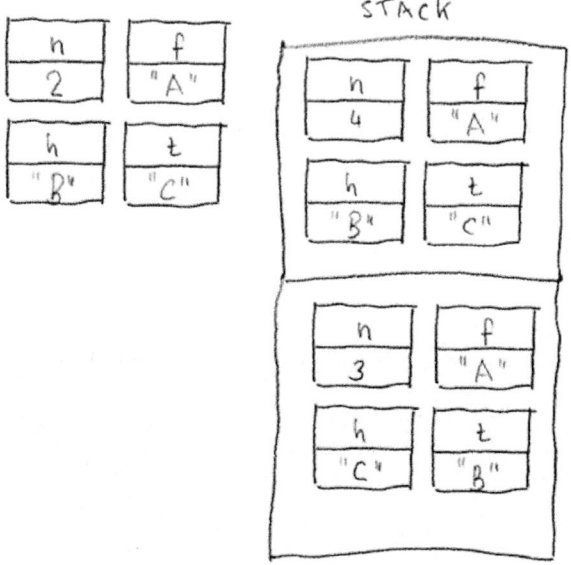

Now after hanoi(2,f,h,t) is finished we restore the old values from the stack and we are back at:

4 Recursion and backtracking

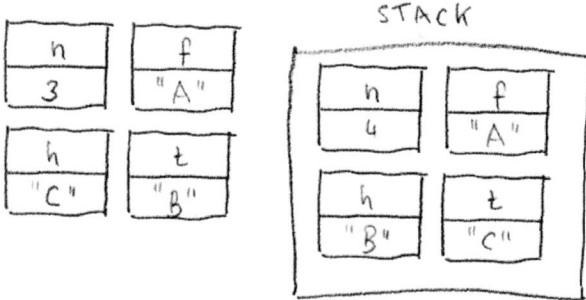

I hope this little example makes it clear why we need a stack even though last-in-first-out is not the way we would organise a supermarket queue. And indeed queues are another data structure.

4.4 Some combinatorics

4.4.1 Factorial

Ok we have chewed on the Hanoi example a lot, let's see some more applications of recursion. Let's do some simple combinatorics: How many ways are there to put 3 students on 3 chairs? Maybe you know the answer: 6 and indeed this is an application of the factorial function, it is $3! = 1 * 2 * 3 = 6$.

But let's pretend we don't know this and let's just derive the function by reasoning and recursion. Ok, if we have 3 students and 3 chairs there are 3 ways to place the first student and then we have 2 students and 2 chairs left.

This smells of recursion. We write fac(n) for the function that calculates the answer. As for Hanoi we need to identify a base case when there is no need for further recursion and as for Hanoi the base case is 0. How many ways are there to place no people on no chairs? No, the answer is not 0. That would mean it is impossible to place no people on no chairs but this is not true. It is easy, just do nothing. There is 1 way to place no people on no chairs. Otherwise, we apply the analysis above

4.4 Some combinatorics

and calculate `n*fac(n-1)`. We end up with the following program:

```
In : def fac(n) :
        if n==0 :
            return 1
        else :
            return n * fac(n-1)

In : fac(3)

Out: 6

In : fac(10)

Out: 3628800
```

Does `fac` always terminate? No, it will crash for negative numbers.

But we didn't need to use recursion, we could have just used a loop

```
In : def fac(n) :
        y = 1
        for i in range(1,n+1) :
            y = i * y
        return y

In : fac(3)

Out: 6

In : fac(10)

Out: 3628800
```

Which one is better? That is a bit of a tricky question. I think the first (recursive) version is prettier but Python isn't very good at executing recursive programs, hence if you care about efficiency then the second program is likely to run faster and use less resources.

87

4 Recursion and backtracking

4.4.2 Binomial coefficents

Here is another combinatorics problem: How many ways are there to draw 6 numbered balls out of 49 if we don't care about the order. Right, this is the question of how many possible combinations are there in Lotto. Maybe again you know the answer, this is called the binomial coefficient and it is written as $\binom{49}{6}$.

Again let's put the formula book away and derive a recursive function just by thinking. Let's look at the ball with the highest number, e.g. 49. We can either take 49 or leave it in the sack. In the first case we still have to draw 6 balls out of 48 while in the 2nd case we need to draw 5 balls out of 48. The number of all the possibilities is simply the sum of these two numbers: $\binom{49}{6} = \binom{48}{6} + \binom{48}{5}$ or in general $\binom{n}{m} = \binom{n-1}{m} + \binom{n-1}{m-1}$

Ok, we have recursion again, but what are the basic cases? Let's not be clever! If we have no balls then it is easy, no matter how many are left, we do nothing and that means there is exactly 1 possibility to draw no balls from any number of balls including 0. That is $\binom{n}{0} = 1$ On the other hand, if we need to draw at least one ball but there are none left then we are stuck and there are no way to complete the task. Hence $\binom{0}{m} = 0$ if $m > 0$.

```
In : def binom(n,m) :
         if m == 0 :
             return 1
         elif n == 0 :
             return 0
         else :
             return binom(n-1,m) + binom(n-1,m-1)

In : binom(49,6)

Out: 13983816
```

Ok, on my computer this actually took a few seconds. Can we solve the problem iteratively (and hence hopefully faster). Indeed, we can reduce `binom` to `fac` and we have already seen how to compute `fac` without recursion.

The idea is the following: in the case of $\binom{49}{6}$: there are 49! ways to order all the balls, and there are 43! ways to order the balls left in the sack and 6! to order the balls we have drawn. Since we don't care about the order of the balls we have drawn or the ones left in the sack the answer is $\frac{49!}{43!6!}$ or in general $\binom{n}{m} = \frac{n!}{(n-m)!m!}$. Hence we come up with the following program:

```
In : def binom(n,m) :
        return fac(n) // (fac(n - m)*fac(m))

In : binom(49,6)

Out: 13983816
```

We get the same answer but faster. Can we always replace recursion by iteration (loops)?

Challenge: Write a solution for Hanoi without Recursion! (Section 4.7)

Question: For which values of m and n does `binom(m,n)` actually works? Is there a difference for the iterative and the recursive solution?

Question: There are some equalities we can use to make `binom` more efficient, e.g. $\binom{m}{m} = 1$ and $\binom{n}{m} = 0$, if $n < m$. Use them to optimise the recursive version of `binom`.

4.5 Solving sudoku: Using backtracking

Next we will show another application of the magic of recursion. We are going to solve some tricky puzzles via a technique called backtracking[1]. Basically we are going to use the

---
[1] https://en.wikipedia.org/wiki/Backtracking

4 Recursion and backtracking

computer to systematically try all possible solutions. Here we exploit that computers can follow instructions very precisely without getting bored and that they are very fast. Hence the approach is very different from a human solving a puzzle.

We use a puzzle called sudoku[2] as an example. Here is an example of a sudoku puzzle:

5	3			7				
6			1	9	5			
	9	8					6	
8				6				3
4			8		3			1
7				2				6
	6					2	8	
			4	1	9			5
				8			7	9

The puzzle is played on a 9 × 9 grid, which is partially filled with numbers 1 − 9, the goal is to complete the grid in such a way that the same number doesn't appear in the same row, in the same column or in the same 3 × 3 square. Hence a solution to the puzzle could look like this:

---

[2]https://en.wikipedia.org/wiki/Sudoku

4.5 Solving sudoku: Using backtracking

5	3	4	6	7	8	9	1	2
6	7	2	1	9	5	3	4	8
1	9	8	3	4	2	5	6	7
8	5	9	7	6	1	4	2	3
4	2	6	8	5	3	7	9	1
7	1	3	9	2	4	8	5	6
9	6	1	5	3	7	2	8	4
2	8	7	4	1	9	6	3	5
3	4	5	2	8	6	1	7	9

Before we get to the actual solver we need to represent the grid and implement some helper functions. To represent the grid we use a list of lists where individual entries represent cells. The number 0 means that the cell is empty.

```
In : grid = [[5,3,0,0,7,0,0,0,0],
             [6,0,0,1,9,5,0,0,0],
             [0,9,8,0,0,0,0,6,0],
             [8,0,0,0,6,0,0,0,3],
             [4,0,0,8,0,3,0,0,1],
             [7,0,0,0,2,0,0,0,6],
             [0,6,0,0,0,0,2,8,0],
             [0,0,0,4,1,9,0,0,5],
             [0,0,0,0,8,0,0,7,9]]
```

Note that we need to specify the line (y) before the column (x), while the usual convention in Mathematics is the other way around.

```
In : grid[2][1]
```

4 Recursion and backtracking

```
Out: 9

In : grid[3][4]

Out: 6
```

Next we need a way to print the grid to be able to display the solution. The default print isn't very readable:

```
In : print(grid)

[[5, 3, 0, 0, 7, 0, 0, 0, 0], [6, 0, 0, 1, 9, 5, 0, 0,
0], [0, 9, 8, 0, 0, 0, 0, 6, 0], [8, 0, 0, 0, 6, 0, 0,
0, 3], [4, 0, 0, 8, 0, 3, 0, 0, 1], [7, 0, 0, 0, 2, 0,
0, 0, 6], [0, 6, 0, 0, 0, 0, 2, 8, 0], [0, 0, 0, 4, 1,
9, 0, 0, 5], [0, 0, 0, 0, 8, 0, 0, 7, 9]]
```

We implement this using two for loops. We don't need to use counters but can iterate directly over the lists.

```
In : def print_grid() :
         for line in grid :
             for square in line :
                 if square == 0 :
                     print(".",end=" ")
                 else :
                     print(square,end=" ")
             print()

In : print_grid()
5 3 . . 7 . . . .
6 . . 1 9 5 . . .
. 9 8 . . . . 6 .
8 . . . 6 . . . 3
4 . . 8 . 3 . . 1
7 . . . 2 . . . 6
. 6 . . . . 2 8 .
. . . 4 1 9 . . 5
. . . . 8 . . 7 9
```

To implement our solver we need to check whether it is possible to place the number n and position (y , x): we implement a function `possible(y,x,n)` which returns `true` if it

4.5 Solving sudoku: Using backtracking

is possible and `false` otherwise. We refer to `grid` as a global variable hence we declare it so that Python doesn't think it is a local variable (it wouldn't actually in this case because we read from the grid and never assign anything).

First we check whether the number appears in the same column:

```
for i in range(0,9) :
    if grid[y][i] == n :
        return False
```

we return `False` if it does, otherwise we continue checking the row in the same way:

```
for i in range(0,9) :
    if grid[i][x] == n :
        return False
```

Now we need to check whether it appears in the same square. This is a bit more tricky. We compute the top left corner of the current square: we first divide both coordinates by 3 ignoring remainder (using //) to find out the relative index of the square, that is a pair of numbers 0 − 2 and then we multiply it by 3 to get the actual coordinate which is 0,3 or 6 for both.

```
x0 = (x//3)*3
y0 = (y//3)*3
```

And then we check each position in the current square by adding a number 0-2 to it using a nested `for`-loop with `range(3)`:

```
for i in range(0,3) :
    for j in range(0,3) :
        if grid[y0+i][x0+j] == n :
            return False
```

If we have passed all the tests without returning `False` we can finally:

93

4 Recursion and backtracking

        return True

Putting everything together we have:

```
In : def possible(y,x,n) :
        global grid
        for i in range(0,9) :
            if grid[y][i] == n :
                return False
        for i in range(0,9) :
            if grid[i][x] == n :
                return False
        x0 = (x//3)*3
        y0 = (y//3)*3
        for i in range(0,3) :
            for j in range(0,3) :
                if grid[y0+i][x0+j] == n :
                    return False
        return True
```

Let's test whether this works.

```
In : print_grid()

5 3 . . 7 . . . .
6 . . 1 9 5 . . .
. 9 8 . . . . 6 .
8 . . . 6 . . . 3
4 . . 8 . 3 . . 1
7 . . . 2 . . . 6
. 6 . . . . 2 8 .
. . . 4 1 9 . . 5
. . . . 8 . . 7 9


In : possible(2,3,2)

Out: True

In : possible(1,1,2)

Out: True

In : possible(1,1,5)

Out: False
```

94

4.5 Solving sudoku: Using backtracking

Now we are ready to implement `solve`. The function has no parameters but operates on the grid which is a global variable. Hence we just call `solve` to try to complete the current `grid`. We look for an empty cell:

```
for y in range(0,9) :
    for x in range(0,9) :
        if grid[y][x] == 0 :
```

if we find one we try to put any digit there.

```
for n in range(1,10) :
    if possible(y,x,n) :
```

If we find a possible digit we put it there:

```
grid[y][x] = n
```

Now we have reduced the problem: there is one less free square and we can call `solve` recursively to fill the remaining grid.

```
solve()
```

What happens next? We return from solve - what could this mean? Ok either we have run into a dead end or we have printed some solution and we are looking for the next one. In either case we **backtrack**, that is, we remove the digit and look for other alternatives.

```
grid[y][x] = 0
```

Now we have tried all the possible digits and exit the loop for n. In this case we return to the caller who can try other alternatives for previous choices.

```
return
```

We only get to this point if there was no empty square (can you see why?). This is actually the trivial case because there is nothing more to do - we have found a solution. All we can do now is to print it.

4 Recursion and backtracking

```
print_grid()
```

There may be several solutions, hence let's pause here and wait for user input.

```
input("More?")
```

Once the user presses return we return, which triggers the search for further solutions. Here is the complete program:

```
In : def solve() :
         global grid
         for y in range(0,9) :
             for x in range(0,9) :
                 if grid[y][x] == 0 :
                     for n in range(1,10) :
                         if possible(y,x,n) :
                             grid[y][x] = n
                             solve()
                             grid[y][x] = 0
                     return
         print_grid()
         input("More?")
```

Let's try it!

```
In : solve()
5 3 4 6 7 8 9 1 2
6 7 2 1 9 5 3 4 8
1 9 8 3 4 2 5 6 7
8 5 9 7 6 1 4 2 3
4 2 6 8 5 3 7 9 1
7 1 3 9 2 4 8 5 6
9 6 1 5 3 7 2 8 4
2 8 7 4 1 9 6 3 5
3 4 5 2 8 6 1 7 9
More?
```

The program returned after we have seen a solution. This means that there was only one solution, which is usually the case for puzzles you find in newspapers or so. We can remove some digits to test that the program can actually find several solutions.

4.5 Solving sudoku: Using backtracking

```
In : grid = [[5,3,0,0,7,0,0,0,0],
             [6,0,0,1,9,5,0,0,0],
             [0,9,8,0,0,0,0,6,0],
             [8,0,0,0,6,0,0,0,3],
             [4,0,0,8,0,3,0,0,1],
             [7,0,0,0,2,0,0,0,6],
             [0,6,0,0,0,0,2,8,0],
             [0,0,0,4,1,9,0,0,5],
             [0,0,0,0,8,0,0,0,0]]

In : solve()

5 3 4 6 7 8 1 9 2
6 7 2 1 9 5 3 4 8
1 9 8 3 4 2 5 6 7
8 5 9 7 6 1 4 2 3
4 2 6 8 5 3 9 7 1
7 1 3 9 2 4 8 5 6
9 6 1 5 3 7 2 8 4
2 8 7 4 1 9 6 3 5
3 4 5 2 8 6 7 1 9
More?
5 3 4 6 7 8 9 1 2
6 7 2 1 9 5 3 4 8
1 9 8 3 4 2 5 6 7
8 5 9 7 6 1 4 2 3
4 2 6 8 5 3 7 9 1
7 1 3 9 2 4 8 5 6
9 6 1 5 3 7 2 8 4
2 8 7 4 1 9 6 3 5
3 4 5 2 8 6 1 7 9
More?
```

In this case there were actually two solutions: the one we had seen already and another one which placed the 7 in a different position.

What happens when we start with an empty board? Can you guess what is the first solution to come up?

Can you modify the program so that it counts the solutions instead of printing them? How many are there on an empty board?

97

4 Recursion and backtracking

4.6 Summary

Recursion is when a function calls itself (directly or indirectly). For recursion to work there have to be some base cases where there are no further recursive calls and each recursive call has to be on a 'simpler' problem.

Recursive functions are excuted via a **stack** where the current values of local variables and parameters are stored and later restored when the recursive call has terminated. Stacks are operated in a last-in first-out (lifo) fashion.

A particular use of recursion is **backtracking** where we systematically try to find the solution of a problem. Either the problem is solved in which case we can print the solution or we try to do a possible move to reduce the problem and call the solver recursively. However, we may end up in a dead end in which case the solver will return, undo a move and try alternative options.

Recursive programs can be replaced by iteration (loops) and in some cases this results in a better performance (mainly because the language doesn't support recursion very well).

4.7 Solution to recursion challenge

There are many clever ways of solving Hanoi iteratively, you can observe that there is some sort of odd-even pattern in the moves and try to come up with a clever formula. Here I am going to present a stupid way to translate a recursive program into an iterative one that always works. We are just going to use a **stack**. So we are just going to copy the way the recursive definition is working. For this purpose it is a good idea to remind ourselves of the recursive definition:

```
In : def hanoi(n,f,h,t):
         if n==0:
             return
         else:
             hanoi(n-1,f,t,h)
             print("Move disk from {} to {}".format(f,t))
             hanoi(n-1,h,f,t)
```

4.7 Solution to recursion challenge

But this time it is not the stack that is built-in to the runtime system of your computer but we are going to use a list. This is a list of tasks and each task is represented as a list again: there are two types:

- the hanoi problem which we represent as `["h",n,f,h,t]` where `n` is the number of disks and `n,f,t` are the names of the poles,
- moving a disk, which is represented as `["m",f,t]` which means move one disk from `f` to `t`.

Initially we start with

```
stack = [["h",n,f,h,t]]
```

If the stack is empty we are done, hence we use a while loop:

```
while stack != [] :
```

Next we take the top level task off the stack:

```
op = stack[0]
stack = stack[1:]
```

We need to check which task we need to perform. It is either a hanoi job:

```
if op[0]=="h" :
```

We assign all the components to variables:

```
n,f,h,t = op[1],op[2],op[3],op[4]
```

and check whether `n` is 0 in which case there is nothing to do:

```
if n==0 :
    continue
```

otherwise we put the tasks corresponding to the recursive call onto the stack:

99

4 Recursion and backtracking

```
else :
    stack = [["h",n-1,f,t,h],
             ["m",f,t],
             ["h",n-1,h,f,t]]+stack
```

we still have to handle the case that it isn't a hanoi job but a move job:

```
elif op[0] == "m" :
    f,t = op[1],op[2]
    print("Move disk from {} to {}"\
          .format(f,t))
```

We omit the else clause since there are only the two possibilities. However, it is good practice to raise an error in this case.

```
In : def hanoi(n,f,h,t) :
         stack = [["h",n,f,h,t]]
         while stack != [] :
             op = stack[0]
             stack = stack[1:]
             if op[0]=="h" :
                 n,f,h,t = op[1],op[2],op[3],op[4]
                 if n==0 :
                     continue
                 else :
                     stack = [["h",n-1,f,t,h],
                              ["m",f,t],
                              ["h",n-1,h,f,t]]+stack
             elif op[0] == "m" :
                 f,t = op[1],op[2]
                 print("Move disc from {} to {}".format(f,t))
```

Let's test it!

```
In : hanoi(4,"A","B","C")

Move disc from A to B
Move disc from A to C
Move disc from B to C
Move disc from A to B
Move disc from C to A
Move disc from C to B
Move disc from A to B
```

```
Move disc from A to C
Move disc from B to C
Move disc from B to A
Move disc from C to A
Move disc from B to C
Move disc from A to B
Move disc from A to C
Move disc from B to C
```

I hope it is clear that by just emulating the stack we can execute any recursive program just using loops.

4.8 Quizzes

We define 4 recursive functions.

```
In : def f0(x) :
        if x==0 :
            return 0
        else :
            return 1+f0(x-1)

In : def f1(x) :
        if x==0 :
            return 0
        else:
            return 1-f1(x+1)

In : def f2(x) :
        if x==0 :
            return 0
        else :
            return 2+f2(x-1)

In : def f3(x) :
        if x==0 :
            return 1
        else :
            return f3(x-1)+f3(x-1)
```

What is the output of the following calls?. Again, please don't use Python but try to figure out the answers just in your head and on paper. The answers in each case are 1,2,3,8,16 or recursion error.

4 Recursion and backtracking

1. f0(4)
2. f1(4)
3. f2(4)
4. f3(4)

4.9 Exercises

1. Write a recursive function `rev` that reverses a list, e.g. `rev([1,2,3])` should return `[3,2,1]`. You can analyse the problem by considering the case that the list is empty and that the list is non-empty. In the latter one you can use recursion to solve the problem. Can you write your function so that it works for strings as well?
2. The Fibonacci series $0, 1, 1, 2, 3, 5, 8, 13, \ldots$ is generated by starting with $0, 1$ and then each subsequent number is the sum of the two previous ones. Write a recursive function `fib(n)` that calculates the nth item of the Fibonacci series starting with 0, e.g. `fib(6)` should return 8. Don't try to be efficient! Actually, how could you be more efficient?
3. Use recursion to calculate the number of shortest paths from the bottom left to the top right corner in an $x \times y$-

grid. E.g. shortest path in a 2×3-grid are:

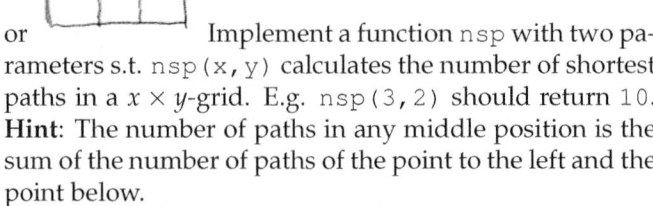

or Implement a function `nsp` with two parameters s.t. `nsp(x,y)` calculates the number of shortest paths in a $x \times y$-grid. E.g. `nsp(3,2)` should return 10. **Hint**: The number of paths in any middle position is the sum of the number of paths of the point to the left and the point below.
4. Use backtracking to calculate the number of **all** paths from the bottom left to the top right corner in a $x \times y$-

4.9 Exercises

grid. This includes path like  Note that every point can only be visited once. Write a function np(x,y) that returns the number of paths in a $x \times y$-grid. E.g. np(2,3) should return 38. **Hint:** Create a grid of booleans where you mark the positions already visited.

5. Implement a Python function that solves the *8 queens puzzle*. The 8 queen puzzle consists of placing 8 queens on a chess board, so that, none of the queens could capture any other. Note that queens can move orthogonally or diagonally in any direction. E.g. a possible solution looks like this:

You should implement a function solve() that when called, it prints the first solution of the puzzle and then it awaits for input. Once the user presses 'enter', the next solution is printed and so on. Hence solve() should produce:

103

4 Recursion and backtracking

```
Q . . . . . . .
. . . . Q . . .
. . . . . . Q .
. . . . . Q . .
. . Q . . . . .
. . . . . . Q .
. Q . . . . . .
. . . Q . . . .
```
more?

- Your program should be able to find all the solutions for the puzzle and each solution only once.
- It should be easy to modify your program, so that, it works for different board sizes.

Hints:

- In any row, there is exactly one queen. Hence, all you need to compute is the column in which each of the 8 queens can be placed.

- You should implement a recursive function `solve(n)` that finds a place for the nth queen and then calls itself recursively for the n+1 queen (unless all the queens have been placed). It should systematically explore all the possibilities using *backtracking*.

- You are allowed (and encouraged) to define extra functions (other than `solve()`) to improve the quality of your code if necessary.

5 Object Oriented Programming

Object Oriented Programming[1] (OOP) is a programming paradigm that was a big deal some time ago, but it is now very well accepted. Python supports multiple programming paradigms, including OOP. Many Python libraries follow this paradigm because it is a very good way to organise code.

The basic idea comes from the 80s and the SmallTalk project[2], and consists of understanding data types as objects in the real world. We (as humans) are capable of categorising things and distinguishing between different types of things. We somehow have our own definition of what an object is (e.g. what a person is), and what is capable of doing (e.g. eat, sleep, breath, etc.). However, everyone of us is an example of that definition, with our particularities (an instance of the class).

In OOP, we mimic the way humans categorise things by denoting these definitions as **classes**, and those examples as **instances** that comply with that definition.

The figure below represent the class `Person` and two instances of this class (`Thorsten` and `Isaac`).

- What defines a person? E.g. name, age, gender, etc (In OOP: we call these 'attributes')

- What can a person do? Sleep, breath, eat, etc. (In OOP, we will call these 'methods')

Instances from the same class will all be able to do the same kind of actions (i.e. methods).

---

[1] https://en.wikipedia.org/wiki/Object-oriented_programming
[2] https://en.wikipedia.org/wiki/Smalltalk

5 Object Oriented Programming

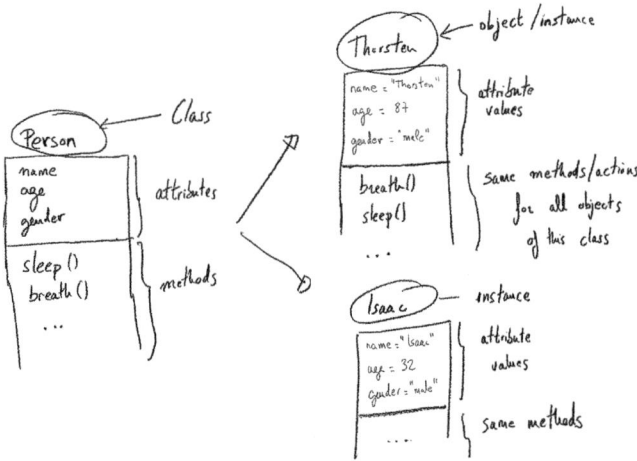

The above figure visually shows the difference between the class definition and two different instances of that class. Note this doesn't represent how Python stores this in memory, this is just a visual description of OOP.

We could also distinguish between different type of people. For example, a student or a professor. They are all persons, that is, they share many of those general things they can do (sleep, breath, etc), but they also have their own roles, and therefore different things that they can do. For example, a student will take exams, but a professor will mark the exams. We could then have classes that inherit from a 'super' class.

If we were to have an instance of class Student, this object will have a name, an age, a gender, but also a year and a course. Students still breath and eat (hopefully), but they also take exams. A professor, however, will not need the attributes year or course (they might teach in different courses!), and we don't take exams any more, but we do a lot of marking.

The figure below represents the two classes Student and Professor and how they both inherit from Person:

5.1 First example: a class for accounts

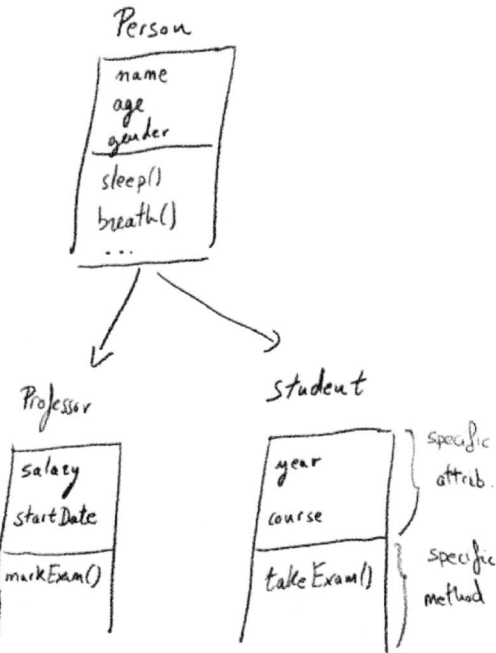

As you may see, this is a very smart way to reduce code duplication if we implement more general operations in 'super'-classes. I will get back to the concept of inheritance later on.

In this chapter you will see plenty of code repetition. As you know, this is a bad programming style. The main purpose of that is to explain step-by-step how we add more functionality to the classes.

5.1 First example: a class for accounts

We are going to create a class that defines what a bank account is, so that, we are capable of creating accounts (objects).

Let's define a class with name Account that does nothing:

```
In : class Account :
        pass # This is Python for doing nothing.
```

107

5 Object Oriented Programming

Similar to functions, we have again used : and indentation to indicate where the class definition block starts. Now that we have a class definition, we can create an instance of that class as follows:

```
In : mine = Account()
```

Basically, what we have done is to call the 'constructor' of the class `Account` (I will get back to this later), to create an object of class `Account` and we assign that to the variable `mine`. What happens if we explore the content of the variable `mine`?:

```
In : mine
Out: <__main__.Account at 0x7f8ff80547f0>
```

Well, it doesn't say much, other than mentioning `Account` and a weird reference. That's the way Python has to refer to objects! Let's check the type of that variable:

```
In : type(mine)
Out: __main__.Account
```

Aha! It once again says this belongs to class `Account`. As I said before, an object may have multiple attributes, and we can define multiple attributes for that object as below. If you have experience with OOP in other languages, the following is going to look weird!

```
In : mine.owner = "Isaac"
```

To access the attributes of an object, we will be using dot '.', and the name of the attribute. In the above case, we have added an attribute `owner` to the object `mine`, and assign the string "Isaac".

Note that as Python is untyped, we are not forced to declare those attributes. This is probably surprising for people with experience on C-like languages like Java or C#, in which the attributes are always declared within the class definition!

Let's add an extra attribute to store the amount of money that the account `mine` has:

5.1 First example: a class for accounts

```
In : mine.amount = 10
```

So, with the simple class definition of Account, we can certainly have multiple objects of the same class, and assign that to multiple variables:

```
In : thorsten = Account()
     thorsten.owner = "Thorsten"
     thorsten.amount = 1
```

Thus, the type of thorsten and mine will be the same (Account), but they refer to two different objects! You may have also noticed that we have 'manually' given the attributes owner and amount to both objects mine and thorsten, and in this way, an object from class Account is not necessarily forced to have the same attributes. I will get back to this later on.

Below you can see a figure representing both objects mine and thorsten, both of them belonging to class Account, but they have their own attributes!

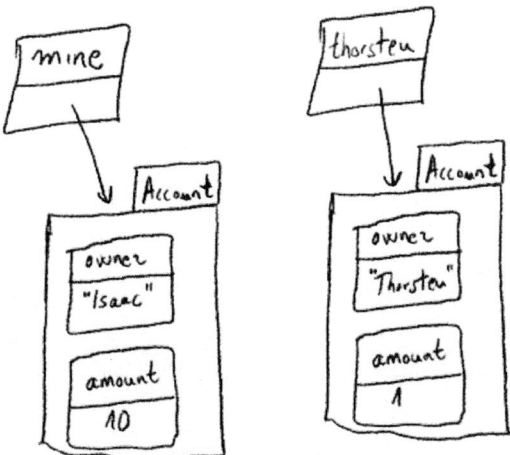

5.1.1 Operations on objects

As mentioned before, objects are capable of performing a number of actions. In OOP, we call them methods, and we can in-

5 Object Oriented Programming

clude those methods within the class definition to tell our program the actions that an object of type `Account` could do. For example, we would like to be able to *withdraw* money from an account:

```
In : class Account :
         def withdraw(self,howmuch) :
             self.amount = self.amount - howmuch
```

Now, the class `Account` contains a method `withdraw` that we have defined in a very similar way we did define functions before! This method will decrease the value of the attribute `amount` by the amount indicated in the parameter `howmuch`.

However, you may have noticed a parameter we called `self`. The name `self` is simply a convention, and you could use whatever you want, but that's not a good practice!

The first argument of every method definition of a class will always be the object **itself**. This allows us to define how this method will be modifying/using a particular object. Funnily enough, you will not normally 'pass' the object as a parameter. Let me show you an example.

As I have redefined the class `Account`, including the new method, I am going to create an object again, and give some values to the attributes `owner` and `amount`:

```
In : thorsten = Account()
     thorsten.owner = "Thorsten"
     thorsten.amount = 1
```

To invoke a method, we will normally do it as follows:

```
In : thorsten.withdraw(100)
```

So, we use the object `thorsten` directly, and then to access the method we use the dot (similar to the way we access attributes), and then we include the parameters of the method, but note that we skipped the first parameter `self`. This might be a bit confusing at first; it is just a shortcut to apply the method to an object, the object is indicated on the left-hand side of the expression.

We can now check the amount of money that the object `thorsten` has:

5.1 First example: a class for accounts

```
In : thorsten.amount

Out: -99
```

Let me do something stupid; what if we create a new object `Another`...

```
In : Another = Account()
```

And we now apply an operation on it?

```
In : Another.withdraw(100)
```

```
 ---------------------------------------------------
 AttributeError Traceback (most recent call last)
 <ipython-input-44-3bc6cacedc45> in <module> --->
 1Another.withdraw(100)
    <ipython-input-39-24e4031eb3b4> in withdraw(self, howmuch)
  1 class Account :     2 def withdraw(self,howmuch) :  --->
 3self.amount = self.amount - howmuch
    AttributeError:  'Account' object has no attribute 'amount'
```

Why did it happen? As Python is an untyped language we don't have to define the attributes of a class... but we should initialise their values, otherwise, `Another` doesn't have an attribute `amount` or `owner`, and that's why we couldn't apply the method `withdraw`.

To deal with this, we typically define a 'constructor' method, called __init__, which is a special type of method that initialises the attributes of a class:

```
In : class Account :
        def __init__(self,owner) :
            self.owner = owner
            self.amount = 0

        def withdraw(self,howmuch) :
            self.amount = self.amount - howmuch
```

What I have done is to create a constructor that receives the name of the owner as a parameter, but the amount is always initialised to 0 (maybe not the best decision, but good for now).

If we now try to create an account object without arguments...

111

5 Object Oriented Programming

```
In : Thorsten = Account()
```

```
   ----------------------------------------------------
   TypeError Traceback (most recent call last)
   <ipython-input-9-03d405de1ddc> in <module>() ---> 1Thorsten =
Account()
   TypeError:    __init__() missing 1 required positional argument:
'owner'
```

Exactly!! It fails!! Why? It did work before! Well, we have now defined the __init__ method, and this will be the method that will be first executed to create a new object, and it now requires one additional parameter. By default, if this method is not specified, the __init__ method is implicitly there, but it doesn't initialise anything.

The correct way to now create an object of class `Account` is like:

```
In : Thorsten = Account("Thorsten")
```

Can we withdraw money from that `Account`?

```
In : Thorsten.withdraw(10)

In : Thorsten.amount

Out: -10
```

Well, we can! We probably shouldn't because the amount was 0 (but that's something else we will improve later).

If you have seen other languages such as Java, you have different types of attributes (public, private, protected, etc) that define the way you can access those values... However, Python is extremely flexible in this sense.

Note that in Python, you can change the values of the attributes in objects, but it's a good policy to use methods to modify their values.

So, the following is possible in Python, but not a good practice!

```
In : Thorsten.amount = Thorsten.amount - 10
```

112

5.1 First example: a class for accounts

```
In : Thorsten.amount

Out: -20
```

We have a method `withdraw`, so, we may also need to have a method to `deposit` money on an account. Let me add that method, and at the same time refactor a bit the code.

```
In : class Account :
         def __init__(self,owner) :
             self.owner = owner
             self.amount = 0

         def withdraw(self,howmuch) :
             self.amount -= howmuch

         def deposit(self,howmuch) :
             self.amount += howmuch
```

We can also add another method to print a 'statement' of the account!

```
In : class Account :
         def __init__(self,owner) :
             self.owner = owner
             self.amount = 0

         def withdraw(self,howmuch) :
             self.amount -= howmuch

         def deposit(self,howmuch) :
             self.amount += howmuch

         def statement(self) :
             return "Owner : {} , Amount : {}"\
                     .format(self.owner, self.amount)
```

Let's create a new object and use the new method `statement` to see amount of money in the account.

```
In : Thorsten = Account("Isaac")

In : Thorsten.statement()

Out: 'Owner : Isaac , Amount : 0'
```

5 Object Oriented Programming

Below you can find a figure representing how the current account definition looks like after adding all the methods above.

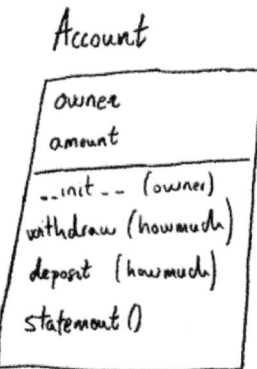

5.1.2 Class variables

Something that annoys me from the previous class definition is that you are allowed to withdraw money even though we haven't got funds. Typically, banks will allow you to withdraw a bit more money than you actually have, but to a certain extent.

To do this, let me introduce the concept of **class variable**. A class variable is a variable that will (typically) be shared amongst all the objects of a particular class. In the example below, I am going to define a class variable `limit` within the class `Account`, and improve the method `withdraw` to ensure that the amount to be withdrawn will not leave the account with a debt higher than the `limit` (for all accounts).

```
In : class Account :
         limit = -1000    # we can define a class variable!

         def __init__(self,owner) :
             self.owner = owner
             self.amount = 0

         def withdraw(self,howmuch) :
```

5.1 First example: a class for accounts

```
        new_amount = self.amount - howmuch
        if new_amount < self.limit:
            print("Sorry, over limit!")
        else:
            self.amount = new_amount

    def deposit(self,howmuch):
        self.amount += howmuch

    def statement(self) :
        return "Owner : {} , Amount : {}"\
               .format(self.owner, self.amount)
```

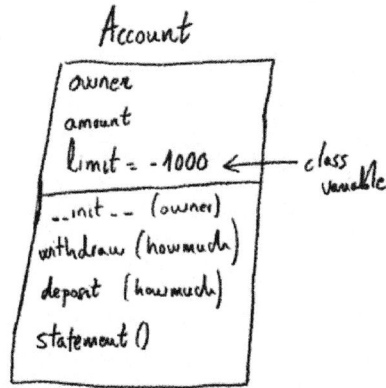

If we now create a new object (remember that amount will be 0), and try to withdraw 1001 pounds:

```
In : Thorsten = Account("Isaac")

In : Thorsten.withdraw(1001)

Sorry, over limit!
```

It works!

```
In : Thorsten.withdraw(1000)

In : Thorsten.statement()
```

115

5 Object Oriented Programming

```
Out: 'Owner : Isaac , Amount : -1000'
```

In the above example, you may have noticed that to access the class variable, we have to use: `self.limit`, similarly to how we access any attribute of the object.

Alternatively, one could use `Account.limit` to access class variables from outside the class definition!

```
In : Account.limit

Out: -1000
```

Something I still don't like from the above class definition is that the `amount` is always set to 0, but I would like to give the programmer the choice to initialise this to a different value, or by default it could be 0. To do so, we can use default parameters (this works for both methods and functions!). Thus, a different way to implement __init__ could be as follows:

```
In : class Account :
        limit = -1000

        # optional parameters
        def __init__(self,owner,amount=0) :
            self.owner = owner
            self.amount = amount

        def withdraw(self,howmuch) :
            new_amount = self.amount - howmuch
            if new_amount < self.limit:
                print("Sorry, over limit!")
            else:
                self.amount = new_amount

        def deposit(self,howmuch):
            self.amount += howmuch

        def statement(self) :
            return "Owner : {} , Amount : {}"\
                    .format(self.owner, self.amount)
```

Now, we can create `Account` objects in two different ways:

```
In : anotherObject = Account("isaac")
```

116

5.1 First example: a class for accounts

This will create an object with `amount=0` because we didn't specify the amount.

```
In : anotherObject.statement()

Out: 'Owner : isaac , Amount : 0'
```

Or you can initialise the amount:

```
In : anotherObject = Account("isaac",100)

In : anotherObject.statement()

Out: 'Owner : isaac , Amount : 100'
```

5.1.3 Inheritance

Inheritance[3] is one of the key concepts that makes OOP very cool and useful. Let me introduce this concept with a simple example.

Imagine that we want to create a different kind of account, e.g., a savings account. This is going to share many of the properties of a standard account, for example, you still have an owner, an amount, you can deposit and withdraw funds. However, we may have something new, for example, an interest rate which will be used to increment your funds.

Thus, we could define a 'subclass' of account that inherits the definition of `Account`, but it contains a class variable `interest_rate`, and an additional function `add_interest` which will allow us to increment the funds in this account according to the `interest_rate`.

In the figure below, I have represented the inheritance from class `Account`, and I have added a class variable `interest_rate` and a method to add interest to the saving account. However, you will not see the attributes `owner` or `amount` in that class definition, because they come directly from the 'super-class' `Account`. You will, however, find a

---
[3] https://en.wikipedia.org/wiki/Inheritance_(object-oriented_programming)

117

5 Object Oriented Programming

method `withdraw` in the definition... why? Well, bear with me, I will get back to that soon.

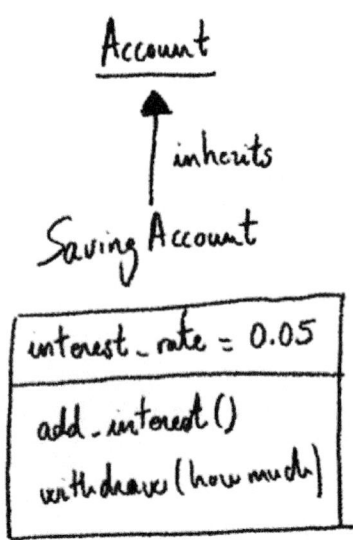

Let's first implement the class and the `add_interest` method.

```
In : class SavingAccount(Account) :
         interest_rate = 0.05

         def add_interest(self) :
             self.deposit(self.amount * self.interest_rate)
```

We can now have an object of this class:

```
In : newSA = SavingAccount("isaac",100)
```

If we check the type:

```
In : type(newSA)
Out: __main__.SavingAccount
```

With this new object, we can do the same operations as you could do with an `Account`, but also we can `add_interest`.

5.1 First example: a class for accounts

```
In : newSA.statement()

Out: 'Owner : isaac , Amount : 100'

In : newSA.add_interest()

In : newSA.statement()

Out: 'Owner : isaac , Amount : 105.0'
```

Can you use this new method on an object of class `Account`?

```
In : Thorsten = Account("Thorsten")
     Thorsten.add_interest()
-------------------------------------------------
AttributeError Traceback (most recent call last)
<ipython-input-37-ad3520b1c601> in <module>  1 Thorsten = Account("Thorsten") ---> 2Thorsten.add_interest()
AttributeError: 'Account' object has no attribute 'add_interest'
```

Of course not!! The object `Thorsten` does not have such a method!

Sometimes, you may want to change the behaviour of a method in the subclass. For example, it is true that we can withdraw funds from a saving account, but there should not be the possibility of an overdraft. Thus, you override the method with a new definition! (but same name!). Let's do this with Python:

```
In : class SavingAccount(Account) :

        interest_rate = 0.05

        def add_interest(self) :
            self.deposit(self.amount * self.interest_rate)

        def withdraw(self,howmuch) :
            if self.amount - howmuch < 0 :
                print("Saving accounts cannot be overdrawn")
            else :
                super(SavingAccount,self).withdraw(howmuch)
```

119

5 Object Oriented Programming

Pay attention to the new definition of the `withdraw` method. I have first checked that the withdrawal will not reduce the amount of money below 0, and in that case I simply print a message saying that saving accounts cannot be overdrawn. Otherwise, if the amount to withdraw `howmuch` is not bigger than `amount`, the `withdraw` method should subtract `howmuch` from the amount (when possible), which is exactly the same behaviour as before. To avoid code repetition, rather than copying the same lines from the `Account` class, that is:

```
new_amount = self.amount - howmuch
if new_amount < self.limit:
    print("Sorry, over limit!")
else:
    self.amount = new_amount
```

I have made use of this:

`super(SavingAccount,self).withdraw(howmuch)`

What does it mean? `super` will check which one is the superclass of `SavingAccount`, and then use the withdraw method from the superclass on `self`.

Alternatively, you could use a static reference to the withdraw method from account, using: `Account.withdraw(self,howmuch)`. Both alternatives are valid, but you may prefer to use one approach or the other depending on how complex is your inheritance!

Static reference to methods is always possible, doing this:

```
In : Account.withdraw(Thorsten, 10)
     Thorsten.statement()

Out: 'Owner : Thorsten , Amount : -20'
```

Which is equivalent to `Thorsten.withdraw(10)`.

5.1.4 The __str__ method

There is a special method called __str__ that Python will use automatically to print an object if this has been implemented in

5.1 First example: a class for accounts

your class. This method needs to have exactly that name (using the double __). This method is meant to return a string!

At the moment, if we print the content of an `Account` object you will see this:

```
In : print(Thorsten)

<__main__.Account object at 0x104419a90>
```

Let's implement the __str__ function to provide a more appealing output! I would like the output to tell me the class name, the owner and the amount, in such a way that it resembles the way we create that object. To do that, I am going to create a class variable with the name of the class.

```
In : class Account :

        class_name = "Account"

        def __init__(self,owner,amount=0) :
            self.owner = owner
            self.amount = amount

        def __str__(self) :
            return "{}('{}',{})"\
                    .format(self.class_name,\
                            self.owner,self.amount)

        def withdraw(self,howmuch) :
            self.amount -= howmuch

        def deposit(self,howmuch) :
            self.amount += howmuch

        def statement(self) :
            return "Owner : {} , Amount : {}"\
                    .format(self.owner, self.amount)

In : Thorsten = Account("Isaac")

In : print(Thorsten)

Account('Isaac',0)
```

121

5 Object Oriented Programming

```
In : Thorsten.deposit(10)

In : print(Thorsten)

Account('Isaac',10)
```

For the `SavingAccount`, we want to the same thing. The question is: do we need to re-implement the __str__ method? Well... not exactly!! We can exploit inheritance in such a way that we simply have to re-define the class variable `class_name`:

```
In : class SavingAccount(Account) :

        interest_rate = 0.05

        class_name = "SavingAccount"

        def add_interest(self) :
            self.deposit(self.amount * self.interest_rate)

        def withdraw(self,howmuch) :
            if self.amount - howmuch < 0 :
                print("Saving accounts cannot be overdrawn")
            else :
                super(SavingAccount,self).withdraw(howmuch)

In : newSA=SavingAccount("Isaac")
     print(newSA)

SavingAccount('Isaac',0)
```

There is actually another way to access the class name, but I wanted to use this as an example of how to use inheritance effectively. We could simply do this:

```
In : Thorsten.__class__.__name__

Out: 'Account'

In : newSA.__class__.__name__

Out: 'SavingAccount'
```

5.2 Example: Implementing Expressions

To illustrate the potential of OOP, we are going to create a program capable of evaluating arithmetic expressions[4]. A mathematical expression is no more than a sequence of numbers and symbols (or at least it looks like it) that follow a number of rules in order to be evaluated consistently.

An expression could be for example: x*y + 7. If we give values to x and y, for example, 2 and 3, respectively, the expression can be evaluated and the result will be 2*3+7 = 13. We evaluated this expression in that way because we know that in maths, we always apply multiplication and division, and then we apply the addition/subtraction.

A different expression is x*(y+7). If we were to evaluate this expression with the previous values, we have 2*(3+7) = 20.

So, with the knowledge you have so far about Python, which data type would you use to 'represent/code' an expression? Most common answer to this: "A string"! Something like this:

```
In : Expr1 = 'x*y+7'
     Expr2 = 'x*(y+7)'
```

But if you thought that (admittedly, I also thought that at first)... Well, you would be wrong!! That would be a very clumsy and annoying way of coding an expression.

Why? Evaluating expressions in such a way would be massively complicated (how would you give a value to x and y to evaluate the expression?)... In addition to that, parentheses would be a nightmare. Actually, parentheses are a lie! They do not really exist in mathematics, but we use them to represent arithmetic expressions in 1 dimension. However, arithmetic expressions are better represented in 2-D as trees! Symbols, constants and variables are nodes of the tree, and arrows indicate their interactions.

We could represent both expression like this:

---

[4]https://en.wikipedia.org/wiki/Expression_(mathematics)

5 Object Oriented Programming

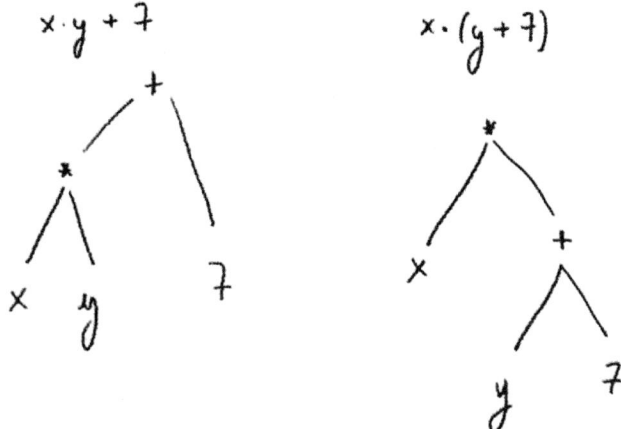

Both trees are totally different, and they uniquely represent both expressions without a doubt. We chose arithmetic expressions as our example for OOP, just for this reason, because they are trees! And we wanted you to learn how to implement trees with OOP. A tree[5] is a data structure widely used in Computer Science. In particular, arithmetic expressions can be represented with a binary tree[6], which is a tree data structure in which each node has at most two children.

Alright, so now that we know what we want to implement, how do we use OOP to create this data structure that will allow us to evaluate expressions?

Let's start thinking about what we need to represent an arithmetic expression such as x*y+7. An `Expression` is composed of different elements. We will need the mathematical symbols, for example + and *, and then we also have variables (e.g. x and y), and constant values (e.g. a number).

Shouldn't we first have a class that defines an expression? something like this:

```
In :  class Expr:
          pass
```

---

[5]https://en.wikipedia.org/wiki/Tree_(data_structure)
[6]https://en.wikipedia.org/wiki/Binary_tree

5.2 Example: Implementing Expressions

Okay, we have the class `Expr` that will be acting as the main class to create expression objects. How do you think symbols +,*, constants and variables should be represented? Attributes? Separated classes?

An expression will be composed of multiple 'sub-expressions' (i.e. sub-trees), for example, a multiplication of two variables (i.e. x*y), but the result of that could be added to a constant value (i.e. 7). If we were to use attributes for that, it wouldn't be flexible enough, we don't know in advance how many sub-expressions/sub-trees we will have for any given expression. Thus, a sensible solution for this is to represent symbols, constants and variable as classes that inherit from the super class `Expr` (as they are all expressions). Something like:

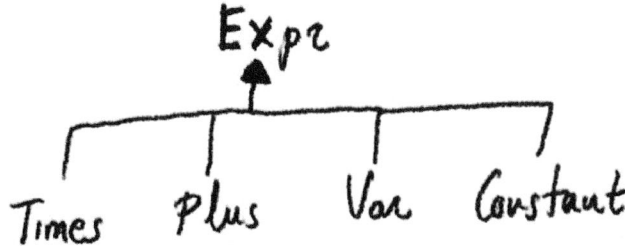

These classes will be basically representing the nodes of the tree.

Okay, let's implement those classes without any content, for now:

```
In : class Times(Expr):
         pass

In : class Plus(Expr):
         pass

In : class Var(Expr):
         pass

In : class Constant(Expr):
         pass
```

125

5 Object Oriented Programming

You might be wondering, do we need something to take care of the parentheses we use in 1 dimension? Well, yes, but for now, let me skip that for a while.

Let's start filling up these classes, with their respective constructor (__init__) methods.

What do we need to represent a constant value? I just said it... we simply need a value. Thus, this could be implemented as:

```
In : class Constant(Expr):

        def __init__(self, val):
            self.val = val
```

In a very similar way, we can implement variables. To represent a variable we need to store its name, which is a string:

```
In : class Var(Expr):

        def __init__(self, name):
            self.name=name
```

These two were easy, but to implement operators (`Plus` and `Times`), what do we need?

We may want to look back at what we actually want to achieve. We want to implement a binary tree which is composed of nodes that have at most two children. Some nodes are 'terminal nodes' (known as leaves) which for arithmetic expressions mean constants or variables (hence why we implemented those with a single value). However, our operator nodes always have two children (one on the left and one on the right). These children could be another operation (i.e. another subtree), or constants/variables (i.e. leaf nodes).

Thus, a possible implementation of the `Plus` and `Times` operators could be as:

```
In : class Plus(Expr):

        def __init__(self,left,right):
            self.left = left
            self.right = right
```

126

5.2 Example: Implementing Expressions

```
class Times(Expr):

    def __init__(self,left,right):
        self.left = left
        self.right = right
```

You might be wondering, what is the type of `left` and `right`? That will depend on the particular expression, but what we know for sure is that they belong to the class `Expr`, they could be of type `Constant, Var, Plus` or `Time`. This is why we have used inheritance here!

Did you like how I defined the `Plus` and `Times` `__init__` methods? They use exactly the same code! And if we were to implement the division or subtraction classes, we would have to repeat that code.

Could we implement that on the super class `Expr`? `Times` and `Plus` are both operations on expressions, but `Constant` and `Var` are also expressions and they have different representations. What we need here is an intermediate class (e.g. `BinOp`) which implements the initialisation for any arithmetic operation (which will always be composed of two sides, left and right).

So, something like this:

```
In : class BinOp(Expr):

        def __init__(self,left, right):
            self.left = left
            self.right = right

    class Times(BinOp):
        pass

    class Plus(BinOp):
        pass
```

Okay, we now have a first implementation of the classes. How do we now write an expression with our classes? Let's create two objects to represent the two expressions we were using before:

127

5 Object Oriented Programming

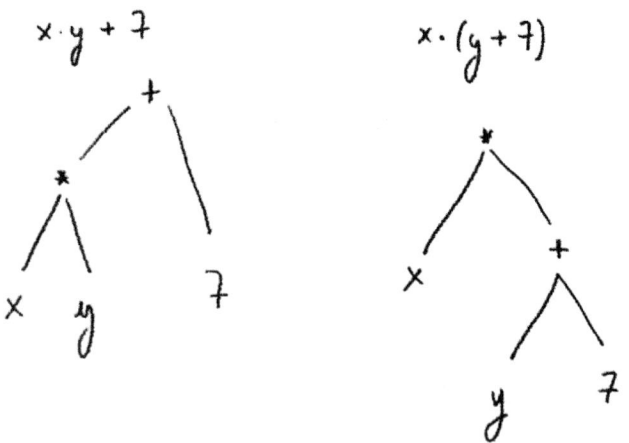

If we want to represent the expression x*y+7, the root node (the node on top of the tree) is a Plus, which is composed of a multiplication on the left, and a constant on the right. The multiplication will have another two children that are variables. So, we could do this as:

```
In : expr1 = Plus(Times(Var("x"),Var("y")),
                  Constant(7))
```

Let's check the types of the nodes what we have on the left and right:

```
In : expr1.left
```

```
Out: <__main__.Times at 0x7f22f05946d8>
```

```
In : expr1.right
```

```
Out: <__main__.Constant at 0x7f22f05946a0>
```

Can we get the name of the variable at the bottom left of the tree?

```
In : expr1.left.left.name
```

```
Out: 'x'
```

5.2 Example: Implementing Expressions

To represent x*(y+7), the root node is now the multiplication.

```
In : expr2 = Times(Var("x"),
                Plus(Var("y"),
                    Constant(7)))

In : expr2.left

Out: <__main__.Var at 0x7f22f0594b00>

In : expr2.left.name

Out: 'x'
```

5.2.1 Printing expressions

Great, we have now a way to represent trees, and they can be as deep as you wish! Let's improve this. I would like to be able to print the expression in 1 dimension. So, we will have to implement the __str__ method for each class (initially I will skip the brackets).

For a Constant, we simply have to print the value. How do we do that? We will need to coerce the type of the value to a string!

```
In : class Constant(Expr):

        def __init__(self, val):
            self.val = val

        def __str__(self):
            return str(self.val)
```

Do we need to do the same for Var? well, the name was already a string, so we just simply return it!

```
In : class Var(Expr):

        def __init__(self, name):
            self.name=name

        def __str__(self):
            return self.name
```

129

5 Object Oriented Programming

I now want to print the operations `Times` and `Plus`. Allow me to start dirty, we will refactor the code later on. We could implement this as:

```
In : class BinOp(Expr):

         def __init__(self,left, right):
             self.left = left
             self.right = right

     class Times(BinOp):

         def __str__(self):
             return str(self.left)+"*"+str(self.right)

     class Plus(BinOp):

         def __str__(self):
             return str(self.left)+"+"+str(self.right)
```

Wait, what have we done there? We have coerced to string what it is on the left and what it is on the right of the expression, and we concatenate the corresponding symbol ("*" or "+"). Funny thing is, we are here applying recursion! When we try to coerce whatever is on the left of the expression, for example, if that is a constant or a variable, well, it will simply use the __str__ method from those classes. If the node corresponds to another operation (sub-expression), it will call this function __str__ once again!

Let me test this with the previous expressions:

```
In : expr1 = Plus(Times(Var("x"),Var("y")),
                  Constant(7))

In : print(expr1)

x*y+7


In : expr2 = Times(Var("x"),
                   Plus(Var("y"),
                        Constant(7)))

In : print(expr2)
```

5.2 Example: Implementing Expressions

```
x*y+7
```

There is a problem right? Where are the brackets? How about this simple solution? We simply add brackets on the __str__ methods of `Times` and `Plus`. Something like this:

```
In : class Times(BinOp):

        def __str__(self):
            return "("+str(self.left)+"*"\
                   +str(self.right)+")"

    class Plus(BinOp):

        def __str__(self):
            return "("+str(self.left)+"+"+\
                   str(self.right) +")"
```

```
In : # x*y+7
     expr1 = Plus(Times(Var("x"),Var("y")),
                  Constant(7))
     #  x*(y+7)
     expr2 = Times(Var("x"),
                   Plus(Var("y"),
                        Constant(7)))

     print(expr1)
     print(expr2)
((x*y)+7)
(x*(y+7))
```

It worked! However, there are way to many brackets!!

Challenge #1: Investigate how to eliminate unnecessary brackets.

Hint: There are some conventions in mathematics (not a rule), preceding rules... for example, times goes first than plus; Those conventions allows us to save brackets (Section 5.5).

5.2.2 Evaluate expressions

So far, we have implemented a way to represent arithmetic expressions using OOP, and we are also able to print them in 1

131

5 Object Oriented Programming

dimension (with a bit too many brackets). Now, we want to add some more functionality to our classes. We want to be able to give a value to the variables of an expression, and evaluate it.

We want to do something like `x=3`, and `y=4`, and then evaluate `expr1` and `expr2` and get the corresponding results.

What sort of object should we use to evaluate these expressions? You shouldn't know the answer to this because we haven't explained that data structure yet. The idea is to have a data structure that allows us to map variable names with values, and what we need for that, is a dictionary[7]!

A dictionary is composed of key-value pairs, so that, if we reference the key, this will provide the value associated to it (this is a mapping between unique keys to values). In our case, the keys are the name of the variables. We are going to use curly brackets to create a dictionary, and we will use square bracket to index each 'key'. Each key-value pair will be separated by commas.

For our example, this could be something like:

```
In : env = {"x" : 3, "y": 4}
```

To get access to the value of 'x', we index it as:

```
In : env["x"]

Out: 3
```

A few things to remember about dictionaries: they are mutable, so that, they can be changed. The values that the keys point to can be any Python value. Dictionaries are not ordered, so the order that the keys are added doesn't necessarily reflect what order they may be reported back.

What we are going to do now is to add a method `eval` to each subclass, to be able to evaluate the entire expression when a dictionary `env` is provided.

---

[7] https://www.Pythonforbeginners.com/dictionary/how-to-use-dictionaries-in-Python%22

5.2 Example: Implementing Expressions

So, for a constant value, the implementation will be straightforward; it will always provide just the value of the constant. However, it might be intuitive that we do require to implement that function, and actually it needs to have the dictionary `env` as an input parameter.

Why? I'll let you think about it.

So the implementation could be as simple as:

```
In : class Constant(Expr):

         def __init__(self,value):
             self.value = value

         def __str__(self):
             return str(self.value)

         def eval(self,env) :
             return self.value
```

For the `Var` class, the `eval` method will actually utilise the dictionary: it will now return the value mapped by the dictionary!

```
In : class Var(Expr):

         def __init__(self,name):
             self.name = name

         def __str__(self):
             return self.name

         def eval(self,env) :
             return env[self.name]
```

So, now that we have used the variable names to look up the assigned values, we can evaluate the classes `Times` and `Plus`. Let's do this in a very simple and dirty way for now, and then we will refactor a bit the code.

```
In : class Times(BinOp):

         def __str__(self):
             return "("+str(self.left)+"*"+\
                    str(self.right)+")"
```

5 Object Oriented Programming

```
        def eval(self,env) :
            return self.left.eval(env)*self.right.eval(env)

    class Plus(BinOp):

        def __str__(self):
            return "("+str(self.left)+"+"+\
                    str(self.right) +")"

        def eval(self,env) :
            return self.left.eval(env)+self.right.eval(env)
```

What we have done is to add a function `eval` to each operation, in which we call recursively the `eval` functions for the `left` and the `right` side of the expression.

Let's test this:

```
In : # x*y +7
     expr1 = Plus(Times(Var("x"), Var("y")), Constant(7))

In : # x * (y+7)
     expr2 = Times(Var("x"), Plus(Var("y"),
                        Constant(7)))

In : env = { "x" : 3 , "y" : 7 }

In : expr1.eval(env)

Out: 28

In : expr2.eval(env)

Out: 42
```

It works well. Will this work for expressions with 3 variables?

```
In : expr3 = Plus(Var("x"),Plus(Var("y"),Var("z")))
     print(expr3)
     expr4 = Plus(Plus(Var("x"),Var("y")),Var("z"))
     print(expr4)
     env = { "x" : 3 , "y" : 7 , "z" : 2}

(x+(y+z))
((x+y)+z)
```

5.2 Example: Implementing Expressions

```
In : expr3.eval(env)

Out: 12

In : expr4.eval(env)

Out: 12
```

Note that the above expressions evaluate to the same number, but they are different trees!

So now we have mostly everything working, let's refactor a bit the code. For example, I don't quite like the idea that `eval` and `__str__` functions of `Times` and `Plus` are almost the same, just changing the actual operator applied. We created the `BinOp` for a reason!

How about this?

```
In : class BinOp(Expr):

        def __init__(self,left, right):
            self.left = left
            self.right = right

        def __str__(self) :
            return "("+str(self.left)+\
                    self.op+str(self.right) +")"

        def eval(self,env) :
            return self.fun(self.left.eval(env),\
                            self.right.eval(env))

    class Times(BinOp):

        op = "*"

        def fun(self,x,y) :
            return x*y

    class Plus(BinOp):

        op = "+"

        def fun(self,x,y) :
            return x+y
```

5 Object Oriented Programming

What we have done is to add an extra class variable with the symbol to print depending on the class (`Times` or `Plus`), and an auxiliary function that performs the operation itself. Let's test it!

```
In : expr1 = Plus(Times(Var("x"), Var("y")), Constant(7))
     print(expr1)

((x*y)+7)
```

5.3 Example: Creating a Knowledge Base

As a second example for OOP, we are going to implement a simple guessing game! But this game will be able to learn from experience, that is, you will be able to teach the program as you play.

For this example, we will create a knowledge base of animals. The user will think of an animal, and the computer will have to figure out which animal it is by asking you (sensible) questions about that animal; the answer will be either yes or no. If it fails to guess correctly the animal, the program will ask you what would be a sensible question to be able to find the right solution next time!

Example 1: The computer only knows how to distinguish between a bird or a cat depending on whether it has 4 legs or not. That is, the initial knowledge base only contains these two animals and one single question.

This could go like this:

```
You: Think of a cat.
Computer: Does it have 4 legs?
You: Yes
Computer: Were you thinking of a cat?
You: Yes
Computer: I knew it!! Let's keep playing!
          I am good at this!
```

5.3 Example: Creating a Knowledge Base

Once again, this follows a tree structure! Depending on whether the user answers yes or no, the computer will ask a different question, or will provide an answer!

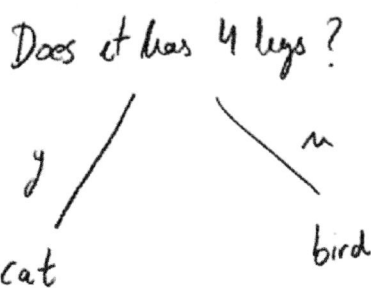

Example 2: You teach the computer a new question.

```
You:   Think of a dog.
Computer: Does it have 4 legs?
You: Yes
Computer: Were you thinking of a cat?
You: No
Computer: What animal were you thinking of?
You: Dog
Computer: What is a question to distinguish
          between dog and cat?
You: Does it bark?
Computer: For dog, what should be the answer?
You: Yes
```

So, now the tree will be updated to include that new question right under the subtree in which the animal has 4 legs. The tree will look like:

5 Object Oriented Programming

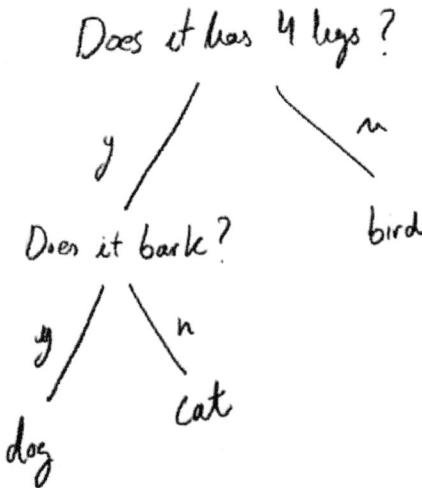

Alright, let's implement this! For now, I will focus on the first example, and we will add the learning capability later.

We are going to start off by creating a super class `Knowledge`, which will not do anything.

```
In : class Knowledge:
         pass
```

Similarly to what we did with the class `Expr`, this class will be representing the entire tree.

What are going to be the nodes of the tree? They are either `Questions` (e.g. "Does it have 4 legs?") or 'final' `Answers` (e.g. Were you thinking of a cat?")

So, we are going to define two classes that inherit from `Knowledge` to implement this game.

```
In : class Question(Knowledge):
         pass

     class Answer(Knowledge):
         pass
```

Let's implement the `__init__` methods for those classes. What do we need for a `Question`?

5.3 Example: Creating a Knowledge Base

We need the text for the question itself (this could be a string with the question); and as this is again a binary tree (yes or no questions), we will have something (another `Question` or an `Answer`) if the user answers yes and if the users replies no.

```
In : class Question(Knowledge):

        def __init__(self, text, ifyes, ifno):
            self.text,self.ifyes,self.ifno = text,ifyes,ifno
```

Remember that in the above code, `ifyes` and `ifno`, could be either of type `Answer` or type `Question`.
What do we need for an `Answer`?
An answer is meant to be a final node, so we only have the actual answer given by the computer!

```
In : class Answer(Knowledge):

        def __init__(self, text):
            self.text = text
```

We can now create our knowledge base. Remember that a `Question` is composed of three different parts, and what we have on the left and the right, could be another question or an answer! Let's create an object with the knowledge base to distinguish between dogs, cats and birds.

For now, the knowledge base will contain the name of the animal. We will add in the learning ability later on.

```
In : kb = Question("Does it have 4 legs?",
           Question("Does it bark?",\
                    Answer("dog"), Answer("cat")),
           Answer("bird"))
```

Alright, we have created the tree. But how do we **play**?
We need to implement a method `play` for both `Question` and `Answer` nodes. The answer to any question will always be either yes (y) or no (n).

So, what I am going to do is to create a very simple function `ask` that will receive the question as an input parameter (a string), read the input from the user (that should be a y or

139

5 Object Oriented Programming

a n), and return `True` or `False` if the answer was yes or no, respectively. Otherwise, we keep asking.

Something like this:

```
In : def ask(q) :
         while True :
             ans = input(q+" ")
             if ans=="y" :
                 return True
             elif ans=="n" :
                 return False
             else :
                 print("Please answer y or n!")
```

Let's now add the `play` methods.

For a `Question` node, we will ask the question itself (so whatever is in `self.text`) and depending on the answer, we will go to the 'yes' or the 'no' branch of the tree, and continue playing! So, `play` will be a recursive function!

```
In : class Question(Knowledge):

         def __init__(self, text, ifyes, ifno):
             self.text,self.ifyes,self.ifno = text,ifyes,ifno

         def play(self):
             if ask(self.text):
                 self.ifyes.play()
             else:
                 self.ifno.play()
```

For an `Answer` node, we just simply need to print our guess (for now).

```
In : class Answer(Knowledge):

         def __init__(self, text):
             self.text = text

         def play(self):
             print("You are thinking of a {}!"\
                 .format(self.text))
```

How do we play then?

So we create again the knowledge base with the same questions and answers as before:

5.3 Example: Creating a Knowledge Base

```
In : kb = Question("Does it have 4 legs?", \
                Question("Does it bark?", \
                        Answer("dog"), Answer("cat")),
                Answer("bird"))
```

And we simply call the method `play` for the `kb` object, which will start from the top node!

```
In : kb.play()

Does it have 4 legs? I don't know
Please answer y or n!
Does it have 4 legs? y
Does it bark? n
You are thinking of a cat!
```

It works!

We now want to make our game smarter, and rather than categorically saying that this is a cat or a dog, it will ask you if the answer is right. In case the guess is incorrect, it will ask the user to provide a question that will let the program identify the animal you were thinking of later on.

So, we need to modify the `play` method; if the guess was right, we haven't got to do much, however, if the answer wasn't right, we need to ask for the animal the user was thinking of first, a question to be able to distinguish that animal in the future, and the answer for that question.

Something like this:

```python
def play(self) :
    if ask("Were you thinking of a {}?"\
           .format(self.text)) :
        print("I knew it!")
    else :
        newanimal = input("What animal were you\
                          thinking of?")
        newquestion = input("What is a question\
                            to distinguish between\
                            {} and {}?".\
                            format(self.text,newanimal))
```

141

5 Object Oriented Programming

```
ask("For {}, what should be the answer?"\
    .format(newanimal))
...
```

But that is incomplete! When we have the information from the user, we need to create the new question and update the knowledge base!

How do we do that? We are not going to modify the tree directly (we could, but it is more complicated), we are going to simply return a tree!!

A simple way to do this is to modify the `play` methods, so that, they will always return the node (or the modified node in case we have a new question to add in the tree). Thus, when we `kb.play()`, this will return the tree.

See the code below which will return a new `Question` node depending if the answer to the question should be yes or not. Note that the animal of that `Answer` node will now be part of the new question!

```
In : class Answer (Knowledge) :

        def __init__(self,text) :
            self.text = text

        def play(self) :
            if ask("Were you thinking of a {}? "\
                    .format(self.text)) :
                print("I knew it!")
                return self      # here we got it right,
                                 # so we simply return the
                                 # Answer node as it is.
            else :
                newanimal = input("What animal were\
                                    you thinking of? ")
                newquestion = input("What is a question\
                                    to distinguish between\
                                    {} and {}? "\
                                    .format(self.text,newanimal))

                # but in case we didn't know the animal
                # we need to modify the node adding
                # the appropriate question and
                # what to do ifyes and if no
```

142

5.3 Example: Creating a Knowledge Base

```
        if ask("For {}, what should be the answer? "\
                .format(newanimal)) :
            return Question(newquestion,\
                            Answer(newanimal),self)
        else :
            return Question(newquestion,\
                            self,Answer(newanimal))
```

For `Question`, we also need to return the node, but this will never change, so, we can simply do this:

```
In : class Question (Knowledge) :

        def __init__(self,text,ifyes,ifno):
            self.text,self.ifyes,self.ifno = text,ifyes,ifno

        #
        def play(self) :
            if ask(self.text) :
                self.ifyes = self.ifyes.play()
            else :
                self.ifno = self.ifno.play()
            return self
```

We want the program to continue running until the user decides to stop playing. To play several times, we need a while loop that will keep asking if the user wants to play or stop.

The knowledge base `kb` will be replaced with the updated tree! Thus, next time we play this should use the name question!

You can see below how it works:

```
In : # I reinitialise the knowledge base,
     # as I have modified the class definitions!
     kb = Question("Does it have 4 legs?",
                   Question("Does it bark?",\
                            Answer("dog"), Answer("cat")),
                   Answer("bird"))

     while True:
         if not ask("Do you want to play?") :
             break
         kb = kb.play()

Do you want to play? y
Does it have 4 legs? y
```

143

5 Object Oriented Programming

```
Does it bark? n
Were you thinking of a cat?  n
Alright, what animal were you thinking of? rabbit
What is a question to distinguish between cat and
rabbit? Does it eat carrots?
For rabbit, what should be the answer?  y
Do you want to play? y
Does it have 4 legs? y
Does it bark? n
Does it eat carrots? y
Were you thinking of a rabbit?  y
I knew it!
Do you want to play? n
```

Excellent! It actually worked!

However, if we now run the above cell, well, the knowledge base will not have the new question (does it eat carrots?); how do we solve this?

We haven't explained how to manipulate files in this book, but we could simply use a library called `pickle` which would allow us to serialise an object. That is, store the data structure on a file, and then read it again!

Remember you can always use the in-line help to see how this module works.

```
In : import pickle
```

Check the help for this library: `help(pickle)`.

Files need to be always opened first; then manipulate them (for example loading their content into a data structure), and finally close them when they are no longer in use.

So, we are going to try to open a file called `animal.kb` in which we will save the tree. The first time we open the file, it will be empty, so we will create our previous knowledge base. To do so, we will use a try-except structure. Why? Whenever we try to open a file that doesn't exist, this will create an exception `FileNotFoundError`. We can simply catch it and create the knowledge base 'manually'.

Then we let the user play, and we keep updating the knowledge base `kb`. At the end of the program, when the user doesn't

5.3 Example: Creating a Knowledge Base

want to play any more, we 'dump' the information contained in kb on the file "animal.kb".

All I said could be coded as:

In : **import pickle**

```
try :
    file = open("animal.kb","rb")
    kb = pickle.load(file)
    file.close()
except FileNotFoundError:
    kb = Question("Does it have 4 legs?",
            Question("Does it bark?",\
                Answer("dog"), Answer("cat")),
            Answer("bird"))

while True :
    if not ask("Do you want to play?") :
        break
    kb = kb.play()

file = open("animal.kb","wb")
pickle.dump(kb,file)
file.close()
```

```
Do you want to play? y
Does it have 4 legs? y
Does it bark? n
Were you thinking of a cat? n
Alright, what animal were you thinking of? rabbit
What is a question to distinguish between cat and
rabbit? Does it eat carrots?
For rabbit, what should be the answer?  y
Do you want to play? n
```

If we now run the code again (I am going to copy paste the previous cell), this should now remember the new question to distinguish rabbits!

In : **import pickle**

```
try :
    file = open("animal.kb","rb")
    kb = pickle.load(file)
    file.close()
```

145

5 Object Oriented Programming

```
    except FileNotFoundError:
        kb = Question("Does it have 4 legs?",
                  Question("Does it bark?",\
                      Answer("dog"), Answer("cat")),
                  Answer("bird"))

    while True :
        if not ask("Do you want to play?") :
            break
        kb = kb.play()

    file = open("animal.kb","wb")
    pickle.dump(kb,file)
    file.close()
```

```
Do you want to play? y
Does it have 4 legs? y
Does it bark? n
Does it eat carrots? y
Were you thinking of a rabbit?  y
I knew it!
Do you want to play? n
```

5.4 Summary

5.4.1 Classes

```
In : class A :
         pass
```

Classes in Python do two things:

- define a new type
- enable us to create objects

5.4.2 Objects

```
In : x = A()
```

Objects are boxes which are created using the class.

146

5.4.3 Attributes (instance variables)

```
In : x.v = 7
```

We can put named variables inside the box. There is no need to declare them. However, it is good practice to access attributes only from inside methods and create them in the constructors.

5.4.4 Methods

```
In : class A :
         def m(self,x) :
             self.y = x+7
In : x = A()
     x.m(3)
     print(x.y)
10
```

A method is very much like a function. Its first argument is always self (you can use another name for it though). When we call a method we use the syntax x.m(3), this finds out where to find the method m using the class of the object x evaluates to. This is an important difference to functions. For functions, we can find out which one is used statically while methods are dispatched dynamically.

5.4.5 Class variables

```
In : class A :
         cv = 7
In : A.cv
Out: 7
In : x = A()
In : x.cv
Out: 7
```

Class variables are shared amongst all objects of a class. Actually methods are a special case of class variables.

5 Object Oriented Programming

5.4.6 Inheritance

```
In : class A :
        def m() :
            pass

     class B (A) :
        def m() :
            pass

     class C (A) :
        def m() :
            A.m()
            super(C,self).m()
```

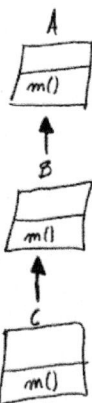

Inheritance is important to factor code, i.e. to avoid code duplication. If there are two classes like B and C above, which have a lot of code in common, it is a good idea to factor this common code out and put it in a common superclass A. We indicate that B and C are subclasses of A. They inherit the methods from A. They can override the methods or modify their behaviours by calling the method from the super class.

5.4.7 Constructors (__init__)

```
In : class A() :
        def __init__(self,v) :
```

148

5.4 Summary

```
            self.v = v
x = A(3)
```

Constructors are special methods which are called when the object is created. In Python, we use a special method called __init__. The double underline indicates that this is an internal method which shouldn't be called explicitly.

5.4.8 Print method (__str__)

```
In : class A() :
         def __init__(self,v) :
             self.v = v

         def __str__(self) :
             return "A({})".format(self.v)

     x = A(3)
     print(x)

A(3)
```

Another standard interface is a print method that creates a readable representation of the object as a string. In Python this method is called __str__. It is called for example by the `str` coercion or by `print`.

5.4.9 Data structures (trees)

```
In : class List :
         pass

     class Nil (List) :
         pass

     class Cons(List) :
         def __init__(self,hd,tl) :
             self.hd,self.tl = hd,tl

     mylist = Cons(1,Cons(2,(Cons(3,Nil))))
```

149

5 Object Oriented Programming

We can use classes to represent data structures. We used classes to represent expression trees, but we could also have used it to create lists (if they wouldn't be already built into Python) as indicated above. We could have implemented a function on lists using the classes above (but much less efficient than the built-in lists in Python).

5.5 Solution to oop challenge

The challenge was to investigate how to eliminate unnecessary brackets.
Hint: There are some conventions in mathematics (not a rule), precedence rules... for example, times goes first than plus; Those conventions allows us to save brackets.

We could apply some precedence rules to get rid of some extra parentheses. Note that in the solution below I started from the code I refactored before, so that, the `BinOp` class will contain the definition of the classes to print and evaluate.

The basic idea is that we assign a level, called precedence to every binary operation. If the precedence is higher the operation binds tighter. So, for example we assign a precedence of 1 to `Plus` and a precedence of 2 to `Times`. The actual numbers are not important, only that higher numbers correspond to tighter binding operators.

If we print a `Plus` expression inside a `Times` we need brackets because we print an operation with a lower precedence inside one with higher precedence like in $3 * (4 + 2)$. On the other hand, if we print an expression with higher precedence inside one with lower precedence we do not need brackets, as for example in $3 * 2 + 4$. Therefore, all we need to check is to compare the precedence of the operation we are about to print with the one within which it is printed, and only add brackets if the own precedence is lower than the one from which we are called.

But, how do we know the precedence of the operator inside which the current expression is printed? We achieve this by adding a new method `str_aux` which is called with the current precedence. In `Expr` we translate a call to `__str__` into

5.5 Solution to oop challenge

self.str_aux(0). Here 0 is the precedence of the top-level and this is the lowest possible precedence because we don't want to add brackets on the outside.

We store the precedence of the operators in a class variable prec which is different for Times and Plus and we implement the idea above uniformly in BinOp. See the final solution below:

```
In : class Expr:

        def __str__(self) :
            return self.str_aux(0)

    class BinOp(Expr):

        def __init__(self,left, right):
            self.left = left
            self.right = right

        def str_aux(self,prec) :
            s = self.left.str_aux(self.prec)+ self.op \
                +self.right.str_aux(self.prec)
            if self.prec < prec :
                return "("+s+")"
            else :
                return s

        def eval(self,env) :
            return self.fun(self.left.eval(env),\
                            self.right.eval(env))

    class Times(BinOp):

        prec = 2
        op = "*"

        def fun(self,x,y) :
            return x*y

    class Plus(BinOp):

        op = "+"
        prec = 1

        def fun(self,x,y) :
            return x+y
```

151

5 Object Oriented Programming

```
class Constant(Expr):

    def __init__(self,value):
        self.value = value

    def str_aux(self,prec):
        return str(self.value)

    def eval(self,env) :
        return self.value

class Var(Expr):

    def __init__(self,name):
        self.name = name

    def str_aux(self,prec):
        return self.name

    def eval(self,env) :
        return env[self.name]


# x*y +7
expr1 = Plus(Times(Var("x"), Var("y")), Constant(7))
print(expr1)

# x * (y+7)
expr2 = Times(Var("x"),
              Plus(Var("y"),
                   Constant(7)))
print(expr2)
```

```
x*y+7
x*(y+7)
```

This code assumes that the expressions are *associative*, i.e. that $(3+4)+4$ is the same as $3+(4+5)$. If this is not the case i.e. for $-$ we also need to print brackets if the precedence is the same.

5.6 Quizzes

Given the following class definitions:

```
In : class Tree :
        def setx(self) :
            self.x=10

    class Node (Tree) :
        def __init__(self,left,right) :
            self.left,self.right = left,right
        def __str__(self) :
            return "({},{})".format(self.left,self.right)

    class Leaf (Tree) :
        def __str__(self) :
            return "()"
```

We create the following object:

```
In : mytree = Node(Node(Leaf(),Leaf()),Leaf())
```

What is the output of the following lines?

```
In : print(mytree)
```

```
In : print(mytree.right.left)
```

```
In : mytree.right = mytree.left
    print(mytree)
```

```
In : mytree.left.setx()
    print(mytree.right.x)
```

```
In : mytree.left = mytree
    print(mytree)
```

5.7 Exercises

Boolean expressions

Your task is to use objects to implement a representation of Boolean expressions which can be printed and evaluated. On top of this, you should implement a method to produce truth

153

5 Object Oriented Programming

tables and a tautology checker which determines whether the expression is **true** for every assignment of truth values.

Exercise 01: You are asked to implement the following classes:

- `Expr` superclass for all boolean expressions,
- `Not` represents logical negation,
- `And` represents logical and,
- `Or` represents logical or,
- `Eq` represents logical equivalence,
- `Var` represents logical variables

with constructors, so that, we can define the following expression trees:

```
e1 = Or(Var("x"),Not(Var("x")))
e2 = Eq(Var("x"),Not(Not(Var("x"))))
e3 = Eq(Not(And(Var("x"),Var("y"))),\
        Or(Not(Var("x")),Not(Var("y"))))
e4 = Eq(Not(And(Var("x"),Var("y"))),\
        And(Not(Var("x")),Not(Var("y"))))
```

Exercise 02: For each class, implement an __str__ method, so that, the above expressions print as follows:

```
x|!x
x==!!x
!(x&y)==!x|!y
!(x&y)==!x&!y
```

It is ok but not perfect if you implement a version that prints too many brackets (that is better than printing not enough).

To minimise the number of brackets you should take into account that:

`Not` (!) binds stronger than `And` (&), e.g.

```
>>> print(And(Not(Var("p")),Var("q")))
!p&q
>>> print(Not(And(Var("p"),Var("q"))))
!(p&q)
```

5.7 Exercises

And (&) binds stronger than Or (|) ,e.g.

```
>>> print(Or(And(Var("p"),Var("q")),Var("r")))
p&q|r
>>> print(And(Var("p"),Or(Var("q"),Var("r"))))
p&(q|r)
```

Or (|) binds stronger than Eq (==),e.g.

```
>>> print(Eq(Or(Var("p"),Var("q")),Var("r")))
p|q==r
>>> print(Or(Var("p"),Eq(Var("q"),Var("r"))))
p|(q==r)
```

This order is transitive, e.g. ! binds stronger than | and ==, and so on.

All binary operations (including ==) are associative, hence there is no need to use brackets when only one kind of operation is used. E.g.

```
>>> print (And(Var("x"),And(Var("y"),Var("z"))))
x&y&z
>>> print (And(And(Var("x"),Var("y")),Var("z")))
x&y&z
```

Exercise 03: Implement a method `make_tt` which returns the truthtable as a string. That is for example `print(e4.make_tt())` should produce the following output:

```
y       | x      | !(x&y)==!x&!y
True    | True   | True
False   | True   | False
True    | False  | False
False   | False  | True
```

The order in which you produce the lines doesn't matter.

The method should work for any collections of variables, not just for two called x and y.

Exercise 04: A proposition is called a tautology if it is always `true`. That is, the truthtable contains only `True` in the last column. Implement a method `isTauto` which determines whether the proposition is a tautology. E.g.

155

5 Object Oriented Programming

```
>>> e1.isTauto()
True
>>> e4.isTauto()
False
```

As above, this method should work correctly for propositions with any collection of variables.

Test your exercises: You can test your code with the examples below. However, it should also work for other examples:

```
In : e1 = Or(Var("x"),Not(Var("x")))
     e2 = Eq(Var("x"),Not(Not(Var("x"))))
     e3 = Eq(Not(And(Var("x"),Var("y"))),\
             Or(Not(Var("x")),Not(Var("y"))))
     e4 = Eq(Not(And(Var("x"),Var("y"))),\
             And(Not(Var("x")),Not(Var("y"))))
     e5 = Eq(Eq(Eq(Var("p"),Var("q")),Var("r")),\
             Eq(Var("p"),Eq(Var("q"),Var("r"))))

     print(e1)
     print(e2)
     print(e3)
     print(e4)
     print(e5)

     print(And(Not(Var("p")),Var("q")))
     print(Not(And(Var("p"),Var("q"))))
     print(Or(And(Var("p"),Var("q")),Var("r")))
     print(And(Var("p"),Or(Var("q"),Var("r"))))
     print(Eq(Or(Var("p"),Var("q")),Var("r")))
     print(Or(Var("p"),Eq(Var("q"),Var("r"))))

     print (e2.eval({"x" : True}))
     print (e3.eval({"x" : True, "y" : True}))
     print (e4.eval({"x" : False, "y" : True}))

     print(e1.make_tt())
     print(e2.make_tt())
     print(e3.make_tt())
     print(e4.make_tt())
     print(e5.make_tt())

     print (And(Var("x"),And(Var("y"),Var("z"))))
     print (And(And(Var("x"),Var("y")),Var("z")))

     print (e1.isTauto())
```

5.7 Exercises

```
print (e2.isTauto())
print (e3.isTauto())
print (e4.isTauto())
print (e5.isTauto())
```

This should produce something like:

```
x|!x
x==!!x
!(x&y)==!x|!y
!(x&y)==!x&!y
p==q==r==p==q==r
!p&q
!(p&q)
p&q|r
p&(q|r)
p|q==r
p|(q==r)
True
True
False
x          | x|!x
True       | True
False      | True

x          | x==!!x
True       | True
False      | True

y          | x        | !(x&y)==!x|!y
True       | True     | True
False      | True     | True
True       | False    | True
False      | False    | True

y          | x        | !(x&y)==!x&!y
True       | True     | True
False      | True     | False
True       | False    | False
False      | False    | True

p          | q        | r        | p==q==r==p==q==r
```

157

5 Object Oriented Programming

```
True    | True   | True   | True
False   | True   | True   | True
True    | False  | True   | True
False   | False  | True   | True
True    | True   | False  | True
False   | True   | False  | True
True    | False  | False  | True
False   | False  | False  | True

x&y&z
x&y&z
True
True
True
False
True
```

6 Functional Programming

As we have seen before, a function in Python is a piece of code that we can call and pass parameters and it may return a value. Some Python functions behave like mathematical functions, like this one:

```
In : def foo(x) :
         return 3*x+1

In : foo(3)

Out: 10
```

Let's call it again!

```
In : foo(3)

Out: 10
```

And, as we would expect from a mathematical function, It returns the same answer.

But others don't behave like this, like this one:

```
In : count = 0
     def incr(x) :
         global count
         count += x
         return count

In : incr(1)

Out: 1
```

Let's call it again!

```
In : incr(1)
```

159

6 Functional Programming

```
Out: 2
```

A mathematical function always returns the same value for the same input, but Python functions like this one doesn't. We are calling functions like `foo` *pure functions* but functions like `incr` impure functions or procedures.

The functional programming style emphasizes the use of pure functions, and indeed there are programming languages like *Haskell* which only use pure functions.

Python is certainly more liberal but it allows us also to program in a functional style. Let's look at some examples.

6.1 Higher order functions and comprehension

You remember the Collatz sequence:

```
In : def collatz(n) :
         while n != 1 :
             print(n,end = ",")
             if n % 2 == 0 :
                 n = n // 2
             else :
                 n = 3 * n + 1
         print(1)

In : collatz(7)

7,22,11,34,17,52,26,13,40,20,10,5,16,8,4,2,1
```

Let's say we want to analyse this sequence and we want to look only at the values divisible by 2, or we want to multiply every element by 3 or we want to do both, i.e. look only at the triples of even elements of the sequence.

We could build this into our `collatz` function but a better and more flexible idea is to construct a list and then process it further.

6.1 Higher order functions and comprehension

```
In : def collatz(n) :
        l = []
        while n != 1 :
            l = l + [n]
            if n % 2 == 0 :
                n = n // 2
            else :
                n = 3 * n + 1
        l=l+[1]
        return l

In : collatz(7)

Out: [7, 22, 11, 34, 17, 52, 26, 13, 40, 20, 10, 5, 16, 8,
      4, 2, 1]
```

Ok, how can we get all the even elements of the list only? Let's first of all define a function that recognizes even numbers:

```
In : def isEven(n) :
        return n%2 == 0

In : isEven(4)

Out: True

In : isEven(3)

Out: False
```

To *filter* out the even element we use the filter function.

```
In : filter(isEven,collatz(7))

Out: <filter at 0x7fdbc924db00>
```

Ok, the result is not very readable but we can fix this by coercing to list (I will explain later why):

```
In : list(filter(isEven,collatz(7)))

Out: [22, 34, 52, 26, 40, 20, 10, 16, 8, 4, 2]
```

The function filter is a bit unusual in that it takes another function in this case isEven as its input. It returns exactly the elements of the list for which the input function returns true.

The other problem was to multiply each element by 3. Ok, let's first define a function that does the multiplication:

161

6 Functional Programming

```
In : def mult3(x) :
        return 3*x

In : mult3(4)

Out: 12
```

To apply the function to each element of the list we use `map`:

```
In : map(mult3,collatz(7))

Out: <map at 0x7fdbc9239f60>
```

Again we need to coerce to be able to read the output:

```
In : list(map(mult3,collatz(7)))

Out: [21, 66, 33, 102, 51, 156, 78, 39, 120, 60, 30, 15, 48,
      24, 12, 6, 3]
```

And now we also see how to combine the two processes:

```
In : list(map(mult3,filter(isEven,collatz(7))))

Out: [66, 102, 156, 78, 120, 60, 30, 48, 24, 12, 6]
```

Note that we only need to apply the `list` coercion in the end. Both `map` and `isEven` work also on the unreadable objects. Indeed, it is better not to use lists because using the objects avoiding to calculate the whole sequence in advance but instead just work with the (unreadable) result of `map`.

Now we want to filter out the numbers divisible by 4 and multiply them by 5. It should be clear what we need to do - the first step is that we define new helper functions. However, we can avoid this cumbersome task (which also involves coming up with a new name each time) by using anonymous functions[1] or lambda functions.

```
In : list(filter(lambda x:x%4==0,collatz(7)))

Out: [52, 40, 20, 16, 8, 4]
```

---
[1] https://en.wikipedia.org/wiki/Anonymous_function

6.1 Higher order functions and comprehension

A lambda function is a short form of a pure function, without a name. We can use it just like a normal named functions, as in:

```
In : (lambda x:x+2)(3)

Out: 5
```

A good way to understand lambda is to say that

```
In : def add2 (x) :
        return x+2
```

is the same as

```
In : add2 = lambda x:x+2
```

Ok then the full expression looks like this:

```
In : list(map(lambda x:x*5,\
         filter(lambda x:x%4==0,collatz(7))))

Out: [260, 200, 100, 80, 40, 20]
```

It is good that we can avoid the names and there are indeed many uses of anonymous functions, indeed the *lambda calculus* (actually λ-calculus) is based on them, but these expressions are getting unreadable quickly.

There is an alternative based on the mathematical notation of *set comprehension*. e.g. to define the set of even numbers we can write

$\{x \mid x \in \mathbb{N} \land x \bmod 2 = 0\}$

Inspired by this we can use list-comprehension:

```
In : [x for x in collatz(7) if x%2 == 0]

Out: [22, 34, 52, 26, 40, 20, 10, 16, 8, 4, 2]
```

This could be read as return the list of all x where x is in the list returned by `collatz(7)` and it is divisible by 2.

Again in Mathematics we also have an easy way to modify the result, that is for example we can define the set of triples of even numbers:

$\{3x \mid x \in \mathbb{N} \land x \bmod 2 = 0\}$

And similar in Python we say:

```
In : [3*x for x in collatz(7) if x%2 == 0]

Out: [66, 102, 156, 78, 120, 60, 30, 48, 24, 12, 6]
```

6 Functional Programming

6.2 Laziness

One of the main selling points of pure functional languages like Haskell is laziness. However, it turns out that there are constructs in Python which allow us to some degree recover this feature.

When using lists we need to compute the whole data structure. This can be horribly inefficient. Let's say we are only interested in the first two elements of the list.

```
In : collatz(7)[0:2]

Out: [7, 22]
```

To calculate the first two elements of a list we first had to calculate the whole list. And actually, we don't even know whether the list is always finite!

This is exactly what the strange unreadable objects where about: they represent iterators which only calculate the objects in a sequence on demand. We can produce iterators using `yield` which returns the next item in the sequence and suspends the current computation. If a consumer of the sequence demands further elements the computation is resumed until the next item is produced.

```
In : def collatz(n) :
        while n != 1 :
            yield n
            if n % 2 == 0 :
                n = n // 2
            else :
                n = 3 * n + 1
        yield 1
```

Now when we run `collatz` we get an unreadable object:

```
In : collatz(7)

Out: <generator object collatz at 0x7fdbc925f390>
```

and as before we can turn it into a list:

```
In : list(collatz(7))
```

6.2 Laziness

```
Out: [7, 22, 11, 34, 17, 52, 26, 13, 40, 20, 10, 5, 16, 8,
      4, 2, 1]
```

But we don't want to do this, we are only interested in the first two elements. Alas `collatz(7)[0:2]` doesn't work, but we need to use a library:

```
In : from itertools import islice

In : list(islice(collatz(7),0,2))

Out: [7, 22]
```

The advantage is that we just computed the part of the sequence we needed and not the rest.

Using `yield` we produce an iterator object. This is exactly what `for` requires. Hence, we can use a `for` loop on the results of `collatz`:

```
In : for x in collatz(7):
         print(x,end=" ")
7 22 11 34 17 52 26 13 40 20 10 5 16 8 4 2 1
```

If you really want to know: an iterator object understands a `next` message and will throw a `stopIteration` exception when there are no elements. So iterators are really objects but they can be used to implement laziness which comes from functional programming. If you want to implement your own iterators[2] (instead of using yield) you need to read up about this protocol.

We can use comprehension on iterators, that is the code from before works without modification:

```
In : [3*x for x in collatz(7) if x%2 == 0]

Out: [66, 102, 156, 78, 120, 60, 30, 48, 24, 12, 6]
```

But hang on: list comprehension returns a list (ok we have sort of indicated this by using [..]). But what if we want to remain lazy and return an iterator? No problem: just replace [..] by (..).

---

[2] https://docs.python.org/3/tutorial/classes.html#iterators

6 Functional Programming

```
In : (3*x for x in collatz(7) if x%2 == 0)

Out: <generator object <genexpr> at 0x7fdbc925fd68>
```

6.3 The sieve of Erathostenes

The sieve of Erathostenes[3] is an ancient way to calculate the prime numbers. You start with all the numbers from 2.

2, 3, 4, 5, 6, 7, 8, 9, 10, 11, 12, 13, 14, 15, 16, 17, 18, 19, 20, 21, 22, 23, 24, 25, 26, 27, 28, 29, 30, 31, 32, 33, 34, 35, 36, 37, 38, 39, 40, 41, 42, 43, 44, 45, 46, 47, 48, 49, ...

Then you take the first number 2 and remove all its multiples:

2, 3, 5, 7, 9, 11, 13, 15, 17, 19, 21, 23, 25, 27, 29, 31, 33, 35, 37, 39, 41, 43, 45, 47, 49, ...

Next we go to the next number which hasn't been removed, that is 3 and remove all its multiples:

2, 3, 5, 7, 11, 13, 17, 19, 23, 25, 29, 31, 35, 37, 41, 43, 47, 49, ...

We continue like this first with 5:

2, 3, 5, 7, 11, 13, 17, 19, 23, 29, 31, 37, 41, 43, 47, 49, ...

and then with 7:

2, 3, 5, 7, 11, 13, 17, 19, 23, 29, 31, 37, 41, 43, 47, ...

When we repeat this process *ad infinitum* (for ever) only the prime numbers are left over.

Using laziness we can implement this process in Python. Surely we cannot calculate all prime numbers but we can construct an infinite stream represented as an iterator that will contain all prime numbers.

Let's start with the stream of all numbers from 2.

```
In : def nats(n) :
         yield n
         yield from nats(n+1)
```

Here we use `yield` again that outputs one element but also `yield from` which merges another stream. To compute the natural numbers starting from n we output n and then we continue with the stream starting from n+1. Let's see:

---
[3] https://en.wikipedia.org/wiki/Sieve_of_Eratosthenes

6.3 The sieve of Erathostenes

```
In : ns = nats(2)

In : next(ns)

Out: 2

In : next(ns)

Out: 3

In : next(ns)

Out: 4
```

I am going to implement a little helper function to go through a stream.

```
In : def show(s) :
        print(next(s),end="\t ")
        if input("More? ")[0]=="y" :
            show(s)

In : ns = nats(2)

In : show(ns)

2         More? y
3         More? y
4         More? y
5         More? y
6         More? n
```

Now to generate the stream of all prime numbers we filter out all the multiples of the first element of the stream (after we have returned it). This can be conveniently done using a comprehension expression.

```
In : def sieve(ns) :
        n = next(ns)
        yield n
        yield from (i for i in sieve(ns) if i%n != 0)
```

Now we can calculate the sequence of all primes:

```
In : primes = sieve(nats(2))
```

6 Functional Programming

and step through it:

```
In : show(primes)

2          More? y
3          More? y
5          More? y
7          More? y
11         More? y
13         More? y
17         More? y
19         More? y
23         More? y
29         More? y
31         More? y
37         More? y
41         More? n
```

6.4 Python in Python

To understand Python better, let's implement a Python interpreter in Python. An interpreter is a program that executes a program.

You may wonder why this is in the chapter on functional programming. One reason is that it didn't fit anywhere else. Another I will explain at the end of the section.

Ok, I am not going for all of Python but a small fragment which I call mini-Python. It should be sufficient to execute the following program that calculates 5×7 using a while loop and addition:

```
In : x = 5
     y = 7
     r = 0
     while not (x == 0) :
         x = x - 1
         r = r + y
     print(r)
```

6.4 Python in Python

First of all we have to represent the syntax of a program. We are going to use trees and we have already seen how to do this in the chapter on OOP. We have statements, blocks and expressions:

```
In : class Statement :
         pass

     class Expression :
         pass

     class Block :
         def __init__(self,stmts) :
             self.stmts = stmts
```

To create a block we need to supply a list of statements. The other classes are *abstract*, we never instantiate them directly but only their subclasses. For expressions we need the following:

```
In : class Const(Expression) :
         def __init__(self,val) :
             self.val = val

     class Var(Expression) :
         def __init__(self,name) :
             self.name = name

     class BinOp(Expression) :
         def __init__(self,e0,e1) :
             self.e0 = e0
             self.e1 = e1

     class Plus(BinOp) :
         pass

     class Minus(BinOp) :
         pass

     class Equal(BinOp) :
         pass

     class Not(Expression) :
         def __init__(self,e) :
             self.e = e
```

As we have seen before, it makes sense to factor out binary

6 Functional Programming

operations. Now in the same vain we can define subclasses for `Statement`:

```
In : class Print (Statement) :
         def __init__(self,e) :
             self.e = e

     class While (Statement) :
         def __init__(self,cond,block) :
             self.cond = cond
             self.block = block

     class Assign (Expression) :
         def __init__(self,var,e) :
             self.var = var
             self.e = e
```

Obviously, we could do much more but I leave this as a challenge. This is enough to translate our example program (we could actually write a program to do this - this is called a 'parser'):

```
In : pgm =\
     Block([Assign("x",Const(5)),
            Assign("y",Const(7)),
            Assign("r",Const(0)),
            While(Not(Equal(Var("x"),Const(0))),
              Block([Assign("x",
                       Minus(Var("x"),Const(1))),
                     Assign("r",
                       Plus(Var("r"),Var("y")))])),
            Print(Var("r"))])
```

Now we have to add methods for the interpreter. For `Expression` we implement a method `eval` which gets a dictionary as an argument. This is very similar to the expressions we have seen before.

```
In : class Const(Expression) :
         def __init__(self,val) :
             self.val = val
         def eval(self,env) :
             return self.val

     class Var(Expression) :
```

170

6.4 Python in Python

```
def __init__(self,name) :
    self.name = name
def eval(self,env) :
    return env[self.name]

class Plus(BinOp) :
    def eval(self,env) :
        return self.e0.eval(env)+self.e1.eval(env)

class Minus(BinOp) :
    def eval(self,env) :
        return self.e0.eval(env)-self.e1.eval(env)

class Equal(BinOp) :
    def eval(self,env) :
        return self.e0.eval(env)==self.e1.eval(env)

class Not(Expression) :
    def __init__(self,e) :
        self.e = e
    def eval(self,env) :
        return not(self.e.eval(env))
```

Let's test this, before we go further. We create an environment:

```
In : env0 = {"x":3,"y":5}
```

And evaluate some expressions:

```
In : Minus(Var("x"),Const(1)).eval(env0)

Out: 2

In : Not(Equal(Var("x"),Const(0))).eval(env0)

Out: True
```

For statements and blocks we implement a `run` method that gets an environment as input and returns the environment after the execution. Running a block means to sequentially execute the statements in it:

```
In : class Block :
        def __init__(self,stmts) :
            self.stmts = stmts
```

171

6 Functional Programming

```
def run(self,env) :
    for s in self.stmts :
        env = s.run(env)
    return env
```

For every type of statement we implement a specific run method:

```
In : class Print (Statement) :
        def __init__(self,e) :
            self.e = e
        def run(self,env) :
            print(self.e.eval(env))
            return env

    class While (Statement) :
        def __init__(self,cond,block) :
            self.cond = cond
            self.block = block
        def run(self,env) :
            while self.cond.eval(env) :
                env = self.block.run(env)
            return env

    class Assign (Expression) :
        def __init__(self,var,e) :
            self.var = var
            self.e = e
        def run(self,env) :
            env[self.var] = self.e.eval(env)
            return env
```

We evaluate the same program but with the modified methods.

```
In : pgm =\
    Block([Assign("x",Const(5)),
        Assign("y",Const(7)),
        Assign("r",Const(0)),
        While(Not(Equal(Var("x"),Const(0))),
            Block([Assign("x",\
                    Minus(Var("x"),Const(1))),
                Assign("r",\
                    Plus(Var("r"),Var("y")))])),
        Print(Var("r"))])

In : pgm.run({})
```

6.4 Python in Python

```
35
```

```
Out: {'x': 0, 'y': 7, 'r': 35}
```

Now what has this to do with functional programming? Clearly our program isn't functional. We update the environment all the time, especially in the code to run `Block` and `While`.

However, we do not rely on the updates and could have replaced them with recursive function calls. In the case of `Block` we process the list using recursion:

```
In : class Block :
         def __init__(self,stmts) :
             self.stmts = stmts
         def run(self,env) :
             if self.stmts == [] :
                 return env
             else :
                 return Block(self.stmts[1:])\
                        .run(self.stmts[0].run(env))

In : class While (Statement) :
         def __init__(self,cond,block) :
             self.cond = cond
             self.block = block
         def run(self,env) :
             if self.cond.eval(env) :
                 return self.run(self.block.run(env))
             else :
                 return env
```

These changes will make our Python program less efficient but this is only because Python doesn't optimize functional code.

But what about assignment? The operation `env[self.var] = ..` changes `env`. However, this doesn't really matter because we never access the *old* value of `env`. Indeed, a clever functional compiler can execute this sort of operation by update without destroying the purely functional behaviours of the program.

It remains `Print`. There is not much we can do about this, because printing is an effect. However, in a purely functional

6 Functional Programming

language effects are modelled by an interface called a monad[4]. The good thing is that using monads one can fine-tune what sort of effects (e.g. updates, input-output, exceptions,...) a program has. To find out more have a look at the functional programming language *Haskell*.

Indeed, the functional version of the program *is* a mathematical semantics of Python programs. We can use it to reason about Python and also verify the correctness of a compiler. Using modern tools like the *Coq* system, proofs can be checked using a computer, actually using a functional programming language with a very powerful type system.

6.5 Challenge: if-then-else

Extend the Python interpreter, such that we can run the following program:

```
n = 0
while n<10 :
if n%2==0 :
    print("*")
else :
    print(n)
n = n + 1
```

That is:

- implement new operators: < and %.
- implement if-then-else

6.6 Summary

Python supports some of the features of functional programming: - Higher order functions

---

[4] https://en.wikipedia.org/wiki/Monad_(functional_programming)

6.7 Solution to the if-then-else challenge

That is functions that take functions as parameters, such as `filter` and `map`. For example `map f l` applies the function `f` to all elements of the list `l` and returns the resulting list.

- lambda notation

We can introduce anonymous functions using the lambda notation, e.g. we can write `lambda x:x+3` for the function that adds 3 to its input.

- Comprehension

This is a notation inspired by set theoretic comprehension that simplifies the use of higher order functions. So for example `[ x for x in l if p(x) ]` returns the list of all elements in `l` for which `p` returns `True`.

- Laziness

This means that we can suspend the computation of a datastructure until it is needed. We can use `yield v` to return v and suspend the computation until further elements are demanded.

We can write an interpreter for Python in a functional style, that provides a mathematical semantics for Python.

6.7 Solution to the if-then-else challenge

We need to implement the following new classes:

```
In : class Lt(BinOp) :
         def eval(self,env) :
             return self.e0.eval(env)<self.e1.eval(env)
     class Mod(BinOp) :
         def eval(self,env) :
             return self.e0.eval(env)%self.e1.eval(env)
     class If (Statement) :
         def __init__(self,cond,ifblock,elseblock) :
             self.cond = cond
             self.ifblock = ifblock
```

175

6 Functional Programming

```
            self.elseblock = elseblock
        def run(self,env) :
            if self.cond.eval(env) :
                return self.ifblock.run(env)
            else :
                return self.elseblock.run(env)
```

Now we need to translate our example program:

```
In : pgm = \
    Block([Assign("n",Const(0)),
        While(Lt(Var("n"),Const(10)),
        Block(
            [If(Equal(Mod(Var("n"),Const(2)),Const(0)),
                Block([Print(Const("*"))]),
                Block([Print(Var("n"))])),
                Assign("n",Plus(Var("n"),Const(1)))])])])
```

And running it gives the expected result:

```
In : pgm.run({})
```

```
*
1
*
3
*
5
*
7
*
9
```

```
Out: {'n': 10}
```

6.8 Quizzes

We initialize the variable `ns`:

```
In : ns = [1,2,3,4]
```

What is the output of the following Python expressions?

1. `list(map(lambda x : 2*x+1,ns))`

2. `list(filter(lambda x : x%2 == 1,ns))`

3. `[ 2*x for x in ns if x%2 == 0]`

4. `[x+y for x in [1,2] for y in [4,6]]`

5. `[x+y for x in [4,6] for y in [1,2]]`

6.9 Exercises

1. Implement the following Python functions calculating lists.

   None of the function should change anything, i.e.they should be free of side-effects (i.e. they are functional.

   - `f1(n)` : returns a list of pairs of subsequent numbers upto n. E.g. `f1(5)` should return

   `[[0, 1], [1, 2], [2, 3], [3, 4], [4, 5]]`

   - `f2(n)` : returns all the lists of increasing numbers upto n-1. E.g. `f2(5)` should return

   `[[], [0], [0, 1], [0, 1, 2], [0, 1, 2, 3]]`

   - `f3(n)` : returns the lists of increasing numbers up to n-1 and then down to 0. `f3(5)` should return

   `[0, 1, 2, 3, 4, 3, 2, 1, 0]`

   - `f4(l)` : returns all the initial sublists of l, e.g. `f4(list("Thor"))` should return

   `[[], ['T'], ['T', 'h'], ['T', 'h', 'o'], ['T', 'h', 'o', 'r']]`

   - `f5(l)` : returns all the lists which can be obtained from l by leaving out elements (the order doesn't matter), e.g. `f4(list("Thor"))` should return `[[], ['r'], ['o'], ['o', 'r'], ['h'], ['h', 'r'], ['h',`

6 Functional Programming

```
           'o'],   ['h', 'o', 'r'],   ['T'],   ['T',
'r'],   ['T', 'o'],   ['T', 'o', 'r'],
['T', 'h'],   ['T', 'h', 'r'],   ['T',
'h', 'o'],   ['T', 'h', 'o', 'r']]
```

2. Define a Python function `fib(x,y)` that calculates the Fibonacci sequence as an iterator. E.g. running `show(fib(1,1))` should produce the following output:

```
1    More? y
1    More? y
2    More? y
3    More? y
5    More? y
8    More? y
13   More? y
21   More? y
34   More? y
55   More? y
89   More? n
```

7 Implementing games with pygame

In this chapter, we are going to learn how to implement games in Python! So far, we have learned the main concepts about programming, including imperative programming, recursion, object oriented programming and functional programming. With those concepts, we are now in a very good position to implement our own game, and to do so, we are going to use a library called **pygame**. Many other libraries are available, but we found this one particularly nice and easy to use!

In our course, we ask the students to implement a game in a group. The group chooses the game, very popular are old arcade games. So far we have only written small programs and only by one person (we hope). The project is a practical introduction to *software engineering*, which involves constructing bigger programs and working together with other people. There is a lot of research going on, but we think it is better just to learn software engineering by doing. Once you realise what the basic issues are, you may be interested to learn more and research different software engineering methodologies.

We choose games because it is easy to see when a game is good - it is fun to play! Also, actually it is quite fun to write a game. We also run a contest to see which group has written the best game.

Hence ideally try to do this assignment as a group but if that is not possible, it is still a good idea to develop a game yourself. However, also the code quality matters for the assessment! Is the code easy to read?, easy to change? and well commented (not too much, not too little)?

Here is some advice how to go about running a software

7 Implementing games with pygame

project:

- Use an online repository with a software maintenance system such as `git`. There are number of free ones like github[1] or bitbucket[2]. They enable you to share the code base, it keeps track of changes and has a number of other useful facilities.
- You need to communicate regularly, for this purpose there are also online sites like slack[3] available which can also be linked to the repository.
- Develop your code in pairs, pairing people with different abilities.
- Don't try to plan every detail but allow some experimentation, play around with prototypes and be prepared to throw code away and rewrite it (refactoring).
- Try to plan a rough schedule which also includes testing and bug fixes.
- Try to make sure that everybody is involved allowing for different level of programming skills.
- Take commitments seriously and don't diverge from agreed specs without consulting the rest of the group.

7.1 What is Pygame?

Pygame[4] is a Free and Open Source Python programming language library for making multimedia applications like games. You might now be wondering, but *What is a library?*

A library is a collection of code (functions and methods that someone else wrote) that we can use in our programs by importing them. We have been doing this before in this book, when we imported the *pickle* library or the *random* library. Most libraries follow the Object Oriented programming paradigm,

---
[1] http://github.com
[2] http://bitbucket.org
[3] http://slack.com
[4] https://www.pygame.org/docs/

7.1 What is Pygame?

so that, we will be able to create objects of different classes, and apply a number of methods on those objects.

You can find the pygame documentation at: `https://www.pygame.org/docs/`, including installation guidelines and the API (Application Programming Interface) with all the functionality of this library.

Important Note: the behaviour of some of the methods we will be using below may differ slightly depending on the Operating System you are running Python.

7.1.1 Installation and basics with pygame

Below we provide a very simple instruction to install **pygame** on your computer. Note that this might not work in all cases, if this doesn't work we refer you to the original pygame guidelines. If you have installed anaconda on your computer, (in most cases) you can simply use `pip` to install the library:

```
pip install pygame
```

Whenever installed, you can use the library on your preferred IDE (i.e. jupyter or Spyder). Having said that, we would recommend you to use spyder for this.

The first step is to import the library and initialise it.

```
In : import pygame
```

```
pygame 1.9.4
Hello from the pygame community.
https://www.pygame.org/contribute.html
```

To make sure that pygame is correctly installed on your computer, you should try to initialise it, running the following instruction:

```
In : pygame.init()
```

```
Out: (6, 0)
```

181

7 Implementing games with pygame

You really want to know what the (6,0) means? Check out the documentation!

When we import a library, we typically have to use the name of the library, before using any of the methods implemented in that library (e.g. pygame.init()). Alternatively, you could import the library as follows:

```
from pygame import init
```

In this way, we could call init directly. Another option is to import everything from pygame:

```
from pygame import *
```

However, this is not really a good practice, because otherwise you may have some clashes (i.e. name of functions on pygame may be the same that those you use in your program). I will be using the first option in this notebook.

To use the library, one of the first things we will need to do is to initialise the display, where we will place/paint things for our game. display is a class defined in the pygame library, which contains various methods. Among them, we can set the size of the display we want to create.

```
In : screen = pygame.display.set_mode((800,400))
```

When we run the above line, you should get a new window that looks like this:

7.1 What is Pygame?

We have also stored the output of running that method on an object `screen`. What is the type of that object? The function display returns an object of class Surface:

```
In : type(screen)

Out: pygame.Surface
```

The `Surface`[5] class provides a good number of methods to do a lot of things.

Our first task will be to fill that screen with a solid colour. Looking at the API, we should use `screen.fill(argument)`, what are the arguments?

For this, we recommend you to use the API, or the in-line help! (Running `help(pygame.Surface.fill)`)

Before using this function, we need to find the class `Color`[6] and see how it works. Run `help(pygame.Color)` to see the documentation of this class.

Ok, we can have an object of class `Color` by simply calling `Color("name")`, where "name" is the name of a colour.

```
In : screen.fill(pygame.Color("red"))

Out: <rect(0, 0, 800, 400)>
```

Anytime that we make some changes on the surface (`screen` object), we need to make it visible; we do this by 'flipping' it.

```
In : pygame.display.flip()
---------------------------------------------------------
NameError Traceback (most recent call last)
<ipython-input-1-d6f4c9bcf213> in <module>() --->
1pygame.display.flip()
   NameError: name 'pygame' is not defined
```

If you run the above cell, you should now see the red background.

---
[5]https://www.pygame.org/docs/ref/surface.html
[6]https://www.pygame.org/docs/ref/color.html

183

7 Implementing games with pygame

However, what's wrong about our program? Have you tried to close the window? Try! you will see we cannot do it! (normally).

To do so, we need to use an event called `quit()`. This instruction will be using a system call to the operating system. We know that this may not work well in some versions of MacOS!

```
In : pygame.quit()
```

The previous line removed the object screen, and we will need to run the previous cells again to create it.

If you are using MacOS, we found the following code useful to close the window:

```
import os

# After the pygame.quit()
os._exit(0)
```

As we don't want that our program finishes immediately after creating the screen, what we need to do is to create a loop that waits for 'events'.

What are pygame events[7]? They are the way to interact with the user.

The event `QUIT` will be triggered when we try to exit the window (using the Operating system cross X).

We are going to create a for loop that reads events from a queue and then analyses them to decide what to do:

The method for that is: `pygame.event.poll()`

We can check the type of the event object returned from that function using the attribute `type`

```
In : screen = pygame.display.set_mode((800,400))
     while True:
         e = pygame.event.poll()
         if e.type == pygame.QUIT :
             break
     quit()
```

---
[7]https://www.pygame.org/docs/ref/event.html

7.2 The Pong Game

With the above cell, you should now be able to close the window when clicking on the cross in the top corner.

Alright, something that already bothers me about the above code, is that we have hard-coded the width and height of the screen. I would rather use of global variables for this:

```
In : WIDTH = 800
     HEIGHT = 400

     screen = pygame.display.set_mode((WIDTH,HEIGHT))
     while True:
         e = pygame.event.poll()
         if e.type == pygame.QUIT :
             break
     quit()
```

7.2 The Pong Game

Alright, so now we are going to implement a very simple game. In particular, we are going to create a reduced version of the game pong[8].

Just for a single player, as if we were playing squash.

Starting from a black background screen, what we want to do first is to draw three borders (the walls).

For that, we are going to *draw* a rectangle[9].

The function `pygame.draw.rect` is expecting a parameter `Rect` (note that class names are case sensitive!) with the specs of the rectangle we want to paint.

In particular, an object of class `Rect` can be created indicating the coordinates for the left top corner of the rectangle, and the desired width and height! You can read more running `help(Rect)`.

The coordinates **(x,y)** indicate the pixels in which the top left corner of every rectangle is. In the figure below, I have drawn the screen, indicating the coordinates for the three rectangles we need to draw the walls.

---

[8] https://en.wikipedia.org/wiki/Pong
[9] https://www.pygame.org/docs/ref/draw.html#pygame.draw.rect

7 Implementing games with pygame

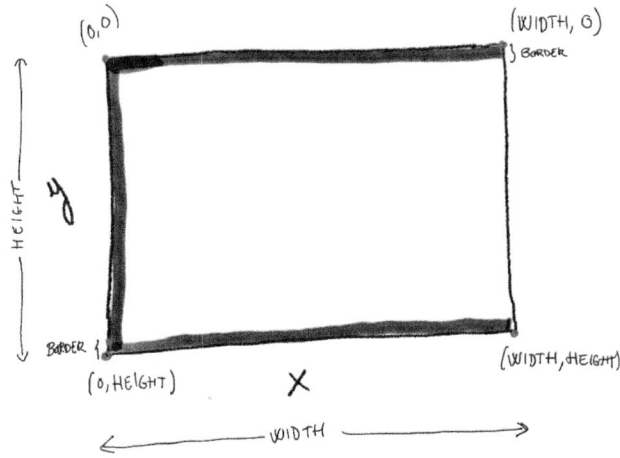

The first rectangle (the one on the top) will start at (0,0), and the width of that rectangle should be equal to the WIDTH of the entire screen. The height of this rectangle, however, should be relatively small, just a few pixels to represent the thickness of the wall.

To do this, we define a new global variable BORDER of size 10 for example. And we are now ready to draw this first rectangle using the `pygame.draw.rect` function, and creating a `Rect` object, starting at (0,0), width =WIDTH, and height = BORDER. Something like:

```
pygame.draw.rect(screen, pygame.Color("white"),\
                 pygame.Rect(0,0,WIDTH, BORDER))
```

The second rectangle (the vertical rectangle on the left of the screen) will also start at (0,0), however, its width should be just the thickness of the wall (i.e. BORDER), and the height of it should be equal to the entire HEIGHT of the screen. So:

```
pygame.draw.rect(screen, pygame.Color("white"),\
                 pygame.Rect(0,0,BORDER, HEIGHT))
```

How about the last rectangle? What are the coordinates? I put in red the coordinates for this rectangle, just above the left

7.2 The Pong Game

bottom corner. The x coordinate can still be 0 (we could move it a bit to the right, but there is not need for that). However, the y coordinate, is all the way down HEIGHT minus the border size! The width of this rectangle will also be equal to the entire WIDTH of the screen, and the height is just the size of the BORDER.

```
pygame.draw.rect(screen, pygame.Color("white"),\
                pygame.Rect(0,HEIGHT-BORDER,WIDTH,\
                BORDER))
```

So, if we put these three lines in our previous code, we end up with something like this: (don't forget to 'flip' after drawing the rectangles! otherwise the changes won't be visible!)

```
In : BORDER = 10

    WIDTH = 800
    HEIGHT = 400


    screen = pygame.display.set_mode((WIDTH,HEIGHT))
    screen.fill(pygame.Color("black"))

    pygame.draw.rect(screen, pygame.Color("white"),\
                pygame.Rect(0,0,WIDTH, BORDER))
    pygame.draw.rect(screen, pygame.Color("white"),\
                pygame.Rect(0,0,BORDER, HEIGHT))
    pygame.draw.rect(screen, pygame.Color("white"),\
                pygame.Rect(0,HEIGHT-BORDER,WIDTH,\
                BORDER))

    pygame.display.flip()
    while True:
        e = pygame.event.poll()
        if e.type == pygame.QUIT :
            break
    quit()
```

This should look like this:

7 Implementing games with pygame

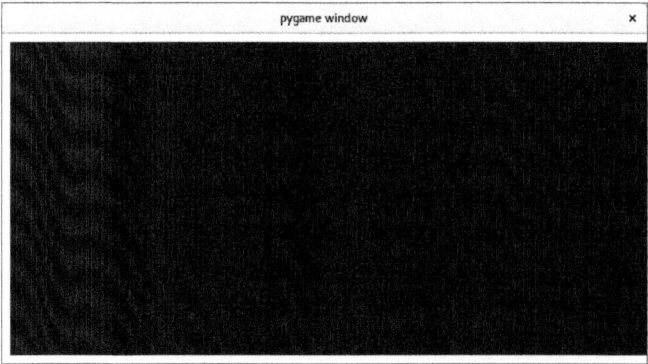

So far, we have simply designed the layout of the game, but now we need to create the **Ball** and the **Paddle** to play the game. Both are 'objects' that will move on the screen, so they are going to have some functionality associated to it. Do you know what we need to do? Yes, we better define a class for `Ball` and one for `Paddle` in which we will code the functionality of both type of objects!

```
In : class Ball:
         pass

     class Paddle:
         pass
```

7.2.1 The Ball class

Within the Ball class, we need to draw a circle this time.

`pygame.draw.circle` draws a circular shape on the Surface. The `pos` argument is the centre of the circle, and radius is the size. The width argument is the thickness to draw the outer edge. If width is zero then the circle will be filled.

An object of class `Ball` will therefore have some coordinates (x,y) which could initialise to some values within the **init** function. The ball will have a given radius, this could be for example a class variable `RADIUS`. So, this could look like this:

```
In : class Ball:
```

188

7.2 The Pong Game

```
RADIUS = 10

def __init__(self, x,y):
    self.x = x
    self.y = y
```

We now want to draw the ball on the coordinates established in `self.x` and `self.y`; what we can do is to add a method `show` that will print the ball in a particular colour (we will see later why this is particularly useful!). Note that this method will be using the pygame.draw.circle method and will act on the `screen` we initialised before. Thus, `screen` is going to be a global variable, and we indicate that specifically in the code as below:

```
In : class Ball:

    RADIUS = 10

    def __init__(self, x,y):
        self.x = x
        self.y = y

    def show(self, colour):
        global screen
        pygame.draw.circle(screen, colour,\
                           (self.x, self.y), self.RADIUS)
```

Alright, we now have the class `Ball` which will allow to create ball objects!

```
ball = Ball(x,y)
```

And right after that, we could use the function `show` to plot it in a given colour (remember this needs to be a `pygame.Color`!

```
ball.show(pygame.Color("white"))
```

Initially, I would like to place the ball on right side, but by the middle, something like:

7 Implementing games with pygame

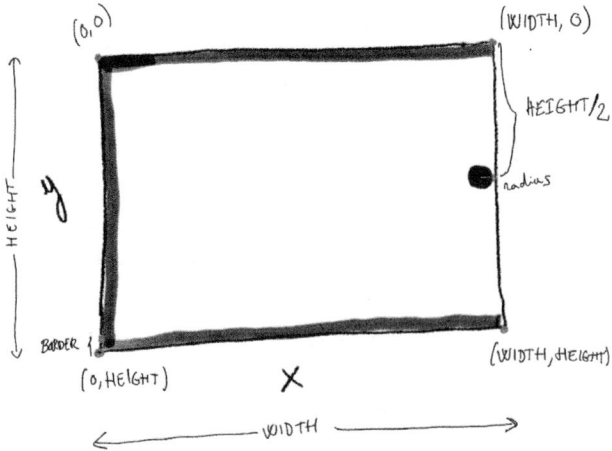

What are the coordinates of the centre of the ball?

- The *x* coordinate is simply the WITDH - the radius of the ball.
- The *y* coordinate is half of the HEIGHT! we will use the operator // to obtain an integer value.

The program could be like this:

```
In : BORDER = 10

    WIDTH = 800
    HEIGHT = 400

    screen = pygame.display.set_mode((WIDTH,HEIGHT))
    screen.fill(pygame.Color("black"))

    pygame.draw.rect(screen, pygame.Color("white"),\
                    pygame.Rect(0,0,WIDTH, BORDER))
    pygame.draw.rect(screen, pygame.Color("white"),\
                    pygame.Rect(0,0,BORDER, HEIGHT))
    pygame.draw.rect(screen, pygame.Color("white"),\
                    pygame.Rect(0,HEIGHT-BORDER,WIDTH,\
                                BORDER))

    ball = Ball(WIDTH-Ball.RADIUS, HEIGHT//2)
    ball.show(pygame.Color("white"))
```

7.2 The Pong Game

```
pygame.display.flip()
while True:
    e = pygame.event.poll()
    if e.type == pygame.QUIT :
        break
quit()
```

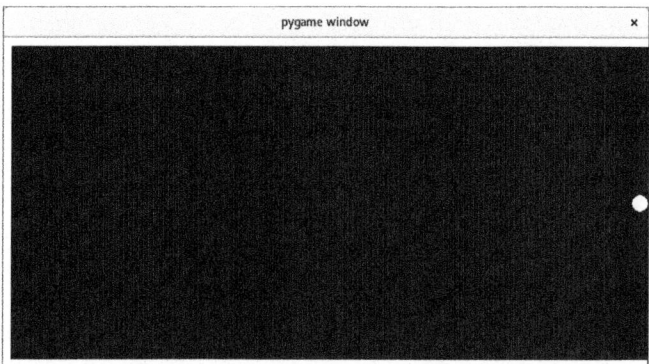

We now have to make the ball move, but how do we do that?

Basically, what we have to do, is to 'remove' the ball from the screen, move it a few pixels and draw it again. For that, we will have to define a `VELOCITY` that will be applied to both X and Y coordinates of the ball to make it move.

Our class `Ball` needs to have two more attributes velocity for x and y coordinates. So we modify the __init__ method to include the velocity for the x axis (`vx`) and the y axis (`vy`).

```
def __init__(self, x,y, vx, vy):
    self.x = x
    self.y = y
    self.vx = vx
    self.vy = vy
```

We also need a method to update the position (i.e. modify `self.x` and `self.y` with the new coordinates). Instead of 'eliminating the ball', how about just setting the colour to black, and then back to white in its new position? This could be something as simple as:

191

7 Implementing games with pygame

```
def update(self):
    # change the colour
    self.show(Color("black"))
    # change position
    self.x = self.x + self.vx
    self.y = self.y + self.vy
    self.show(Color("white"))
```

Thus, the class will be like this:

```
In : class Ball:

    RADIUS = 10

    def __init__(self, x,y, vx, vy):
        self.x = x
        self.y = y
        self.vx = vx
        self.vy = vy

    def show(self, colour):
        global screen
        pygame.draw.circle(screen, colour,\
                          (self.x, self.y),\
                          self.RADIUS)

    def update(self):
        # change the colour
        self.show(pygame.Color("black"))
        # change position
        self.x = self.x + self.vx
        self.y = self.y + self.vy
        self.show(pygame.Color("white"))
```

So now, we have to create the object `ball` with the new class definition, and add a `VELOCITY`.

Once again, this will be a global variable; what is a good value for `VELOCITY`? Well, that depends on what we want the ball to do. Let's say I just simply want to move the ball from right to left horizontally.

As we want to move on the x-axis, from right to left, what we need is a value for `VELOCITY` that will decrement the x position of the ball. So this value must be negative. I am going to try something like -4 to see what it does. The velocity in the y-axis

7.2 The Pong Game

will be set to 0! as I don't want this to draw a diagonal, but to go horizontally.

```
ball = Ball(WIDTH-Ball.RADIUS, HEIGHT//2,\
            -VELOCITY, 0)
```

How do we make it move? well, we could call the update method within the while loop. Note that whenever we run this update method, it should be followed by a `display.flip()`, otherwise, we will not see any change!

```
while True:
    e = pygame.event.poll()
    if e.type == pygame.QUIT :
        break
    ball.update()
    pygame.display.flip()
```

The program could be like this: (it should do something funny!)

```
In : BORDER = 10

    WIDTH = 800
    HEIGHT = 400
    VELOCITY = 4

    screen = pygame.display.set_mode((WIDTH,HEIGHT))
    screen.fill(pygame.Color("black"))

    pygame.draw.rect(screen, pygame.Color("white"),\
                    pygame.Rect(0,0,WIDTH, BORDER))
    pygame.draw.rect(screen, pygame.Color("white"),\
                    pygame.Rect(0,0,BORDER, HEIGHT))
    pygame.draw.rect(screen, pygame.Color("white"),\
                    pygame.Rect(0,HEIGHT-BORDER,WIDTH,\
                    BORDER))

    ball = Ball(WIDTH-Ball.RADIUS, HEIGHT//2,\
                -VELOCITY, 0)
    ball.show(pygame.Color("white"))

    pygame.display.flip()
    while True:
```

7 Implementing games with pygame

```
    e = pygame.event.poll()
    if e.type == pygame.QUIT :
        break
    ball.update()
    pygame.display.flip()
quit()
```

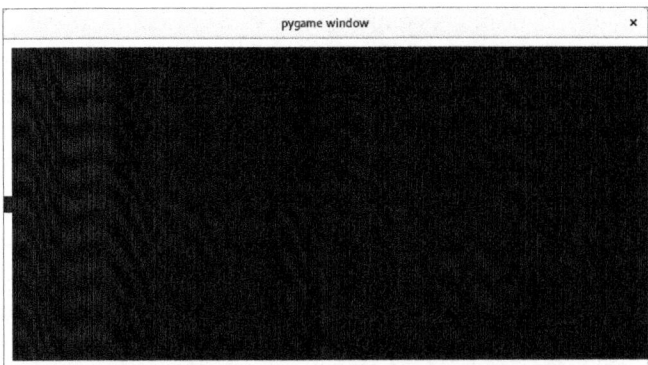

Wow, that went fast!! and it clashed immediately with the left wall, leaving a back hole!

Alright, how do we prevent this from happening? In other words, I want that the ball to bounce back when it touches one of the borders! What I am saying is basically we want to change the sign of the velocity whenever it clashes with a border, which is, whenever the current coordinates + the increment in velocity (either `vx` or `vy`) will make it clash.

First thing I would do in the `update` function is to compute the new coordinates x and y before painting it. Something like this:

```
newx = self.x + self.vx
newy = self.y + self.vy
```

Now, I would check if the `newx` and the `newy` are colliding with the borders.

- For the x axis, this would be easy. Whenever `newx` is less than BORDER size, we have touched it!

7.2 The Pong Game

```
if newx < BORDER:
    self.vx = -self.vx
```

- For the y axis, we need to check it doesn't collide with the top and bottom walls!

```
if  newy < BORDER or newy > HEIGHT-BORDER:
    self.vy = -self.vy
```

Putting everything together, the function could look like this:

```
def update(self):

    newx = self.x + self.vx
    newy = self.y + self.vy

    if newy < BORDER or newy > HEIGHT-BORDER:
        self.vy = -self.vy
    elif newx < BORDER:
        self.vx = -self.vx
    else:
        # change the colour
        self.show(pygame.Color("black"))
        self.x = self.x + self.vx
        self.y = self.y + self.vy
        self.show(pygame.Color("white"))
```

Let me put everything together again here:

```
In : class Ball:

    RADIUS = 10

    def __init__(self, x,y, vx, vy):
        self.x = x
        self.y = y
        self.vx = vx
        self.vy = vy

    def show(self, colour):
        global screen
        pygame.draw.circle(screen, colour,\
                          (self.x, self.y),\
```

195

7 Implementing games with pygame

```
                    self.RADIUS)

    def update(self):
        newx = self.x + self.vx
        newy = self.y + self.vy

        if newy < BORDER or newy > HEIGHT-BORDER:
            self.vy = -self.vy
        elif newx < BORDER:
            self.vx = -self.vx
        else:
            # change the colour
            self.show(pygame.Color("black"))
            self.x = self.x + self.vx
            self.y = self.y + self.vy
            self.show(pygame.Color("white"))

BORDER = 10

WIDTH = 800
HEIGHT = 400
VELOCITY = 10

screen = pygame.display.set_mode((WIDTH,HEIGHT))
screen.fill(pygame.Color("black"))

pygame.draw.rect(screen, pygame.Color("white"),\
                 pygame.Rect(0,0,WIDTH, BORDER))
pygame.draw.rect(screen, pygame.Color("white"),\
                 pygame.Rect(0,0,BORDER, HEIGHT))
pygame.draw.rect(screen, pygame.Color("white"),\
                 pygame.Rect(0,HEIGHT-BORDER,WIDTH,\
                             BORDER))

ball = Ball(WIDTH-Ball.RADIUS, HEIGHT//2,\
            -VELOCITY, 0)
ball.show(pygame.Color("white"))

pygame.display.flip()
while True:
    e = pygame.event.poll()
    if e.type == pygame.QUIT :
        break
    ball.update()
    pygame.display.flip()
quit()
```

7.2 The Pong Game

If you run the above cell, well, it is kind of fun! it does reverse, however, we forgot to account for the radius of the ball! We need to slightly modify the conditions to add the radius:

```
def update(self):

    if newy+Ball.RADIUS > HEIGHT-BORDER \
         or newy-Ball.RADIUS < BORDER :
        self.vy = -self.vy
    elif newx-Ball.RADIUS < BORDER :
        self.vx = -self.vx
    else:
        # change the colour
        self.show(Color("black"))
        self.x = newx
        self.y = newy
        self.show(Color("white"))
```

7.2.2 The Paddle class

So now we are tasked to implement the Paddle, a few things to keep in mind for this:

- The paddle will be always in the same 'x' position, we only move it up and down
- The movement needs to be managed with the mouse (new type of event)
- We need to define its width and height
- Note that when we draw a rectangle we need to provide Top-left coordinates, however, to centre the Paddle on the screen, we need to compute its centre.

For now, I am going to simply create the class `Paddle`, and initialise any attributes. As I just said, we only need to move the paddle along the y axis, this means we only need the *y* attribute. The paddle will have its own width and height, so as we did with the `Ball`, these attributes will be class variables:

```
class Paddle:
    WIDTH = 10
```

197

7 Implementing games with pygame

```
HEIGHT = 80

def __init__(self, y):
    self.y = y
```

Now we have to draw the rectangle representing the paddle. Similar to what we did before, we are going to create a `show` method that will be using `pygame.draw.rect` to draw it. Annoyingly, to draw the rectangle we need to provide the coordinates of the top left corner, but in `self.y` what we want to represent is the centre of the paddle.

To get the paddle initially centred: (this might get confusing! I recommend you to have a look at the figure I prepared below)

- The x coordinate will be the WIDTH of the screen minus the WIDTH of the Paddle (Paddle.WIDTH)
- The y coordinate will be the current position (self.y) minus half of the HEIGHT of the paddle

```
pygame.draw.rect(screen, colour,\
                 pygame.Rect(WIDTH-self.WIDTH,\
                 self.y-self.HEIGHT//2,\
                 self.WIDTH,self.HEIGHT))
```

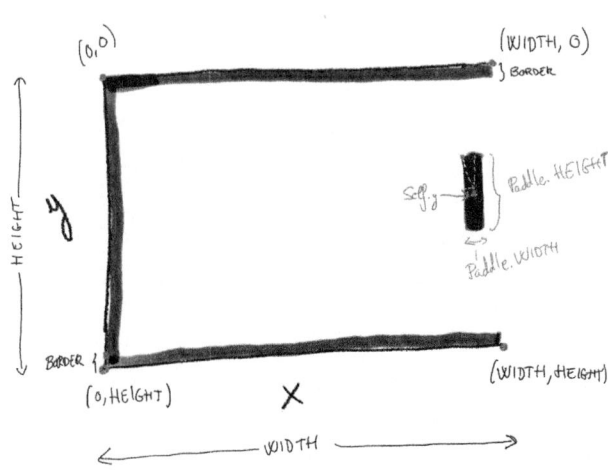

7.2 The Pong Game

Putting everything together:

```
In : class Paddle:
         WIDTH = 10
         HEIGHT = 80

         def __init__(self, y):
             self.y = y

         def show(self, colour):
             global screen
             pygame.draw.rect(screen, colour,\
                             pygame.Rect(WIDTH-self.WIDTH,\
                             self.y-self.HEIGHT//2,\
                             self.WIDTH,\
                             self.HEIGHT))
```

We could now simply plot the paddle creating an object of the class, as we did before with the ball.

```
In : paddle = Paddle(HEIGHT//2) # we put it in the middle
     paddle.show(pygame.Color("white"))
```

We now have to move the paddle! We will need to revisit the `Ball` class to check collisions with the paddle.

We want to play the game with the mouse, and pygame provides that functionality![10].

If we look at the documentation, we can get the position of the mouse with `pygame.mouse.get_pos()`. This will provide a tuple (x,y) with the coordinates of the mouse. We simply need to use that to update the position of the paddle. Once again, we are going to create an `update` method that will hide the paddle, update its position, now based on the mouse position, and then show the paddle in its new position.

```
def update(self) :
    self.show(Color("black"))
    # check where the mouse is.
    self.y = pygame.mouse.get_pos()[1]
    self.show(Color("white"))
```

---

[10]https://www.pygame.org/docs/ref/mouse.html

199

7 Implementing games with pygame

As before, we need to include call the update method within the while loop to make it happen!

```
while True :
    e = pygame.event.poll()
    if e.type == pygame.QUIT :
        break
    ball.update()
    paddle.update()
    pygame.display.flip()
```

So our game so far is like this:

In :
```
import pygame

class Ball:

    RADIUS = 10

    def __init__(self,x,y,vx,vy):
        self.x=x
        self.y=y
        self.vx=vx
        self.vy=vy


    def show(self,colour):
        global screen
        pygame.draw.circle(screen, colour,\
                           (self.x,self.y), Ball.RADIUS)

    def update(self):

        newx= self.x+self.vx
        newy= self.y+self.vy

        if newx < BORDER+Ball.RADIUS:
            self.vx = -self.vx
        elif newy < BORDER+Ball.RADIUS or \
        newy > HEIGHT-BORDER-Ball.RADIUS:
            self.vy = -self.vy
        else:
            self.show(pygame.Color("black"))
            self.x= newx
            self.y= newy
            self.show(pygame.Color("white"))
```

7.2 The Pong Game

```
class Paddle:

    WIDTH= 20
    HEIGHT= 80

    def __init__(self,y):
        self.y = y

    def show(self, colour):
        global screen
        pygame.draw.rect(screen, colour,\
                    pygame.Rect(WIDTH-self.WIDTH,\
                            self.y-self.HEIGHT//2,\
                            self.WIDTH,\
                            self.HEIGHT))

    def update(self):
        self.show(pygame.Color("black"))
        self.y = pygame.mouse.get_pos()[1]
        self.show(pygame.Color("white"))

WIDTH = 800
HEIGHT = 400
BORDER = 20
VELOCITY = 4

pygame.init()

screen = pygame.display.set_mode((WIDTH,HEIGHT))

screen.fill(pygame.Color("black"))

pygame.draw.rect(screen, pygame.Color("white"),\
            pygame.Rect(0,0,WIDTH,BORDER))
pygame.draw.rect(screen, pygame.Color("white"),\
            pygame.Rect(0,0,BORDER,HEIGHT))
pygame.draw.rect(screen, pygame.Color("white"),\
            pygame.Rect(0,HEIGHT-BORDER, WIDTH,\
                    BORDER))

ball = Ball(WIDTH-Ball.RADIUS, HEIGHT//2,\
            -VELOCITY,-VELOCITY)
ball.show(pygame.Color("white"))

paddle = Paddle(HEIGHT//2)
```

7 Implementing games with pygame

```
paddle.show(pygame.Color("white"))

while True:
    e = pygame.event.poll()
    if e.type == pygame.QUIT:
        break
    ball.update()
    paddle.update()
    pygame.display.flip()
pygame.quit()
```

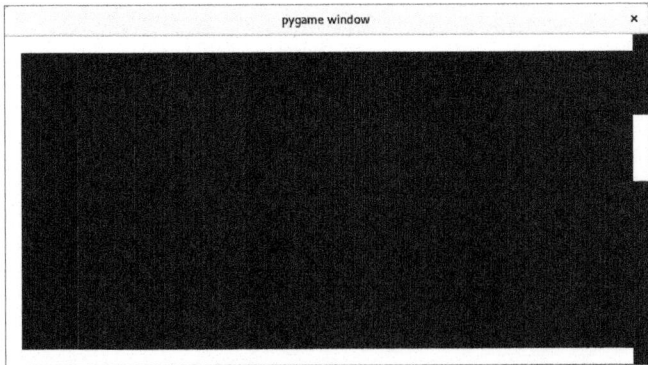

So far, this works, but there are a few things that we need to fix. - The paddle clashes with the borders - The ball doesn't stop when hit by the paddle!

As we did before with the ball, we need to check that whenever we are going to update the position of the object, it doesn't collide with the borders. In this case, we only need to check with the top and bottom walls, and whenever the user moves further than those points, there won't be any update. However, we need to remember that the position we are storing (self.y) is the centre of the paddle.

```
    def update(self) :
        newy = mouse.get_pos()[1]
        if newy-self.HEIGHT//2 >= BORDER \
            and newy+self.HEIGHT//2 <= HEIGHT-BORDER :
            self.show(pygame.Color("black"))
            self.y = newy
            self.show(pygame.Color("white"))
```

7.2 The Pong Game

Something I didn't realise before is that the ball should be next to the paddle. So, I am going to move the original position of the ball slightly to the left to avoid initial collision with the paddle. Also, as we have now controlled the collision with the borders, I am going to set both initial velocities (`vx` and `vy`) with negative values to make the ball goes in a diagonal!

```
ball = Ball(WIDTH-Ball.RADIUS-Paddle.WIDTH,\
            HEIGHT//2, -VELOCITY,-VELOCITY)
ball.show(pygame.Color("white"))
```

We also have to check where the paddle is on the `Ball` class to prevent collisions. For simplicity, the (object) `paddle` will be used here as a global variable.

We need to add an extra condition that if the `newx` of the ball (+ its radius) is greater than the x position of the Paddle (remember it remained fixed at WIDTH-Paddle.WIDTH), and (at the same time) the `newy` makes it collide with the paddle, the velocity should be reversed, so that, we simulate that bouncing.

As we are using `paddle` as a global variable, `paddle.y` will give us the current centre of the paddle, whenever `newy` is above or below half the height of the paddle (Paddle.HEIGHT//2), this means they are colliding!

The easiest way to calculate that is to check if the absolute difference between the paddle centre and the ball is less than half of the paddle height:

```
...
elif newx+Ball.RADIUS >= WIDTH-Paddle.WIDTH \
    and abs(newy-paddle.y) <= Paddle.HEIGHT//2 :
        self.vx = - self.vx
...
```

So, the update method in `Ball` will now look like this:

```
class Ball:
    ....
    def update(self):
        # change the colour
```

203

7 Implementing games with pygame

```
        newx = self.x + self.vx
        newy = self.y + self.vy

        if newy+Ball.RADIUS > HEIGHT-BORDER \
            or newy-Ball.RADIUS < BORDER :
            self.vy = -self.vy
        elif newx-Ball.RADIUS < BORDER :
            self.vx = -self.vx
        elif newx+Ball.RADIUS >= WIDTH-Paddle.WIDTH \
            and abs(newy-paddle.y) <= Paddle.HEIGHT//2 :
            self.vx = - self.vx
            # REPEATED CODE: How do we solve it? :-)
        else:
            # change position
            self.show(pygame.Color("black"))
            self.x= newx
            self.y= newy
            self.show(pygame.Color("white"))
```

Something that annoys me a bit is that the ball starts moving immediately after the program runs, and I would rather wait for the user to click with the mouse (or the keyboard) and the the ball starts moving. How do we do this?

We could add an extra attribute `moving` to the ball that indicates with True or False if the Ball should move. The `update` method won't do anything if this variable is not set to True.

```
class Ball:

    RADIUS = 10

    def __init__(self,x,y,vx,vy) :
        self.x = x
        self.y = y
        self.vx = vx
        self.vy = vy
        self.moving = False

    def update(self) :
        if not self.moving :
```

7.2 The Pong Game

```
return
# .. rest of the code below
```

Then we need to include a new event type[11] (`MOUSEBUTTONDOWN`) to capture the click of the user.

Whenever the user clicks the mouse, the variable `moving` will be set to True:

```
while True :
    e = pygame.event.poll()
    if e.type == pygame.QUIT :
        break
    elif e.type == pygame.MOUSEBUTTONDOWN :
        ball.moving = True
    ball.update()
    paddle.update()
    pygame.display.flip()
```

Task: How would you use the mouse click to start and pause the game?

7.2.3 Adding Lives and Score display

What else can we do to make our game nicer?

We could count the number of successful hits to the ball, and also have a number of lives, so that, the game is over if we miss the ball a number of times.

To do this, you could have two global variables:

```
lives = 5
score = 0
```

On class `Ball`, we could modify the `update` method, so that, whenever we hit the ball, we increase that score. But if we miss it, we will lose one life. In addition, if we have lost, I would like to re-initialise the position of the Ball (waiting again for the click of the user); we could just simply call the **init** method!

---

[11]https://www.pygame.org/docs/ref/event.html

205

7 Implementing games with pygame

```
elif newx+Ball.RADIUS >= WIDTH-Paddle.WIDTH:
    if abs(newy-paddle.y)<=Paddle.HEIGHT//2:
        self.vx = -self.vx
        score += 1
    else:       # or we missed it!
        lives -= 1
        # reinitialise the position of the ball!
        self.show(pygame.Color("Black"))
        self.__init__(WIDTH-Ball.RADIUS-Paddle.WIDTH, \
                      HEIGHT//2,-VELOCITY,-VELOCITY)
        self.show(pygame.Color("White"))
```

We could then print the values of lives and points in the terminal, something like this:

```
while True:
    print ("lives ={}, points = {} "\
            .format(lives, score))
    if lives < 0: # game OVER!
        break

    e = pygame.event.poll()
    if e.type == pygame.QUIT:
        break
    elif e.type == pygame.MOUSEBUTTONDOWN :
        ball.moving = True

    ball.update()
    paddle.update()
    pygame.display.flip()
pygame.quit()
```

However, this is going to be very slow, and each iteration of the while loop is printing off a line. Why don't we try to do this nicer, and display those values on the game?

We need a function `show` that takes some text and print it on the screen. This is surprisingly difficult - here is the recipe:

- We first need to set the font style that we will use, see font[12].

---
[12]https://www.pygame.org/docs/ref/font.html

7.2 The Pong Game

```
pygame.font.SysFont(font.get_default_font(),15)
```
- Render the String using `Font.render`[13].

This creates a new Surface with the specified text rendered on it. pygame provides no way to directly draw text on an existing Surface: instead you must use Font.render() to create an image (Surface) of the text, then blit this image onto another Surface.

- Show that on the Surface using blit[14], i.e. draw an image onto another.

```
screen.blit(surf,(0,0))
```

```
In : def show(text):
        pygame.font.init()
        myFont = pygame.font.\
        SysFont(pygame.font.get_default_font(),25)
        surf = myFont.render(text, False,\
                            pygame.Color("black"),\
                            pygame.Color("white"))
        screen.blit(surf, (0,0))
```

With this, we could now call this function in every iteration:

```
while True:
    show("lives ={}, points = {} "\
        .format(lives, score))
    if lives < 0: # game OVER!
        break

    e = pygame.event.poll()
    if e.type == pygame.QUIT:
        break
    elif e.type == pygame.MOUSEBUTTONDOWN :
        ball.moving = True

    ball.update()
    paddle.update()
    pygame.display.flip()
pygame.quit()
```

---
[13]https://www.pygame.org/docs/ref/font.html#pygame.font.Font.render
[14]https://www.pygame.org/docs/ref/surface.html?highlight=blit#pygame.Surface.blit

7.2.4 Adding Sounds

Pygame also allows us to add sounds into the game with `pygame.mixer.Sound`[15].

We create an object of type mixer, that reads a music file from the drive:

```
In : pong = pygame.mixer.Sound("pong.wav")
```

Then, we could play the sound whenever the ball hits the paddle or the walls, by using:

```
pong.play()
```

I am going to let you decide where to put that line of code :-)

7.2.5 Adjusting the speed of the ball

If you run the same game on a Windows operating system, the ball will move very fast, and you want the same speed on all devices, you need to use a clock[16].

```
FRAMERATE = 50

clock = time.Clock()

while True:
    show("lives ={}, points = {} "\
        .format(lives, score))
    if lives < 0: # game OVER!
        break

    e = pygame.event.poll()
    if e.type == pygame.QUIT:
        break
    elif e.type == pygame.MOUSEBUTTONDOWN :
        ball.moving = not ball.moving
```

---

[15] https://www.pygame.org/docs/ref/mixer.html#pygame.mixer.Sound
[16] https://www.pygame.org/docs/ref/time.html#pygame.time.Clock

7.2 The Pong Game

```
    ball.update()
    paddle.update()
    clock.tick(FRAMERATE)
    pygame.display.flip()
pygame.quit()
```

Why does it happen? Each iteration of the loop is called a frame. To ensure that the game runs the same way independently of your operating system and your computer, we added the line `clock.tick(FRAMERATE)` which is locking the frame rate to 50 frames per second. Thus, we have avoided the game to run at different speeds depending on the speed of the machine.

The final game will look like this:

```
In : import pygame

    class Ball:

        RADIUS = 10

        def __init__(self,x,y,vx,vy):
            self.x=x
            self.y=y
            self.vx=vx
            self.vy=vy
            self.moving = False


        def show(self,colour):
            global screen
            pygame.draw.circle(screen, colour,\
                              (self.x,self.y),\
                              Ball.RADIUS)

        def update(self):
            global lives, score

            if not self.moving:
                return

            newx= self.x+self.vx
            newy= self.y+self.vy
```

209

7 Implementing games with pygame

```
        if newx < BORDER+Ball.RADIUS:
            pong.play()
            self.vx = -self.vx
        elif newy < BORDER+Ball.RADIUS or \
        newy > HEIGHT-BORDER-Ball.RADIUS:
            pong.play()
            self.vy = -self.vy
        elif newx+Ball.RADIUS > WIDTH-Paddle.WIDTH:
            if abs(newy -paddle.y) <= Paddle.HEIGHT//2 :
                score += 1
                pong.play()
                self.vx = -self.vx
            else: # we missed the ball
                lives-=1
                self.show(pygame.Color("black"))
                self.__init__(WIDTH-Ball.RADIUS-\
                              Paddle.WIDTH,
                              HEIGHT//2,\
                              -VELOCITY,-VELOCITY)
                self.show(pygame.Color("white"))
        else:
            self.show(pygame.Color("black"))
            self.x= newx
            self.y= newy
            self.show(pygame.Color("white"))


class Paddle:

    WIDTH= 20
    HEIGHT= 80

    def __init__(self,y):
        self.y = y

    def show(self, colour):
        global screen
        pygame.draw.rect(screen, colour,\
                        pygame.Rect(WIDTH-self.WIDTH,\
                                    self.y-self.HEIGHT//2,\
                                    self.WIDTH,\
                                    self.HEIGHT))

    def update(self):
        newy = pygame.mouse.get_pos()[1]

        if newy >= BORDER+self.HEIGHT//2\
```

210

7.2 The Pong Game

```
        and newy <= HEIGHT- BORDER-self.HEIGHT//2 :
            self.show(pygame.Color("black"))
            self.y = newy
            self.show(pygame.Color("white"))


WIDTH = 800
HEIGHT = 400
BORDER = 20
VELOCITY = 4

FRAMERATE = 50

lives = 5
score = 0


def show(text):
    pygame.font.init()
    myFont = pygame.font.\
    SysFont(pygame.font.get_default_font(),25)
    surf = myFont.render(text, False,\
                    pygame.Color("black"),\
                    pygame.Color("white"))
    screen.blit(surf, (0,0))


pygame.init()

screen = pygame.display.set_mode((WIDTH,HEIGHT))

screen.fill(pygame.Color("black"))

pygame.draw.rect(screen, pygame.Color("white"),\
            pygame.Rect(0,0,WIDTH,BORDER))
pygame.draw.rect(screen, pygame.Color("white"),\
            pygame.Rect(0,0,BORDER,HEIGHT))
pygame.draw.rect(screen, pygame.Color("white"),\
            pygame.Rect(0,HEIGHT-BORDER, WIDTH,\
                    BORDER))

ball = Ball(WIDTH-Ball.RADIUS-Paddle.WIDTH,\
        HEIGHT//2, -VELOCITY,-VELOCITY)
ball.show(pygame.Color("white"))

paddle = Paddle(HEIGHT//2)
```

7 Implementing games with pygame

```
paddle.show(pygame.Color("white"))

pong = pygame.mixer.Sound("pong.wav")

clock = pygame.time.Clock()

while True:
    show ("Lives {}, Score {}".format(lives,score))

    if lives <1:
        break

    e = pygame.event.poll()
    if e.type == pygame.QUIT:
        break
    elif e.type == pygame.MOUSEBUTTONDOWN:
        ball.moving = not ball.moving

    clock.tick(FRAMERATE)
    ball.update()
    paddle.update()
    pygame.display.flip()
pygame.quit()
```

```
pygame 1.9.4
Hello from the pygame community.
https://www.pygame.org/contribute.html
```

This implementation of the game uses only very basic features of pygame. By using some more advanced classes, e.g. `sprites` we could have automatised the collision detection.

7.3 Project

Develop a simple game in a group of 3-4 people. The game should include a graphical interactive component and it is suggested that you use the pygame API. E.g. you may implement an arcade game like tetris or space invaders.

While it is a good idea to look at code samples please do not use other people's code but write your own! Please be explicit

7.3 Project

about ideas/structures you have learned from other people's code.

Try to address the following goals:

1. Quality of game play

    - Is the game fun to play?
    - Does it look and sound good?
    - Is it free from errors?
    - Is it platform independent (i.e does it run on mac, windows and linux) ?

2. Software quality

    - Good use of Python (objects, functions etc)
    - Reusable code
    - Is the code well documented?

3. Other factors

    - Did the team work well together?
    - Are the instructions clear?
    - Did the demo go well?
    - Clear references to code used for inspiration
    - Good use of tools (e.g. git)

8 Getting started with Data Science

The use of data science[1] techniques has become a very hot topic nowadays due to their ability to extract useful knowledge from data. In this chapter, we aim to provide a brief example of data science with Python. So, we are not aiming at developing another comprehensive introduction to data science (as there are many other courses for that), but to show that with the concepts you have learned on this book about programming, you will be able to use third-party libraries very easily and be a step closer to perform your own data analysis.

In this chapter, we are going to make use of the **Pandas** library for data structures, and the **Scikit-learn** library to perform data mining.

8.1 Data analysis with the Pandas library

Pandas[2] is a Python library for data manipulation and analysis, which is widely used to perform data mining and machine learning.

In data science, we typically represent data as a table with a number of rows (e.g. instances or observations), and columns (which contain features of those observations), and we will perform some analysis on them. For example:

---
[1] https://en.wikipedia.org/wiki/Data_science
[2] https://en.wikipedia.org/wiki/Pandas_(software)

8 Getting started with Data Science

In the above table, we have a dataset with two instances, and five attributes about them. These attributes are basic information about the instances, and for example, I included an additional attribute `Risk` which indicates if there is any risk involved in lending money to that individual!

We typically store this kind of table in `.csv`, or `.xlsx` formats.

Pandas offers data structures and classes that make reading this kind of data very easy. In particular, Pandas provides two main data structures: `Series` and `DataFrame`. `Series` is a 1-dimensional array **where all the elements belong to the same type**. A `DataFrame`[3] is a 2-dimensional data structure (a table), which can be accessed by the name of the column. Thus, a `DataFrame` can be seen as a dictionary of `Series` instances.

Actually, we can create a `DataFrame` from a dictionary. We have used dictionaries as a way to establish a relationship between key-value pairs. The above table could be represented as:

```
In : d = {'Name': ["Thorsten", "Isaac"],\
          'Age': [45,32],\
          'Profession':["Lecturer","Lecturer"],
```

---

[3]https://pandas.pydata.org/pandas-docs/version/0.23.4/generated/pandas.DataFrame.html

8.1 Data analysis with the Pandas library

```
                'Nationality': ["German","Spanish"],\
                'Risk': [True, False]}

In : d

Out: {'Name': ['Thorsten', 'Isaac'],
       'Age': [45, 32],
       'Profession': ['Lecturer', 'Lecturer'],
       'Nationality': ['German', 'Spanish'],
       'Risk': [True, False]}
```

To access the series of values under each key, we simply use the name of the key, for example:

```
In : d['Name']

Out: ['Thorsten', 'Isaac']
```

To create a data frame we need to first import the Pandas library, and then call the constructor of the class `DataFrame` passing the dictionary as input data. In most Pandas tutorials, you will see that the Pandas library is imported like this:

```
In : import pandas as pd
```

In this way, rather than using the full name (something like `df = pandas.DataFrame(data=d)`), we can simply write:

```
In : df = pd.DataFrame(data=d)

In : df

Out:       Name  Age  Profession  Nationality   Risk
      0  Thorsten   45    Lecturer       German   True
      1     Isaac   32    Lecturer      Spanish  False
```

As you can see, when printing a `DataFrame` object, we get a very nice formatted table. On the jupyter notebook, the column names will be highlighted in bold.

Let's check the type of this `df` variable:

```
In : type(df)

Out: pandas.core.frame.DataFrame
```

8 Getting started with Data Science

So, what is the advantage of using data frames rather than using dictionaries? Well, Pandas has implemented a great number of functions that can be applied on the data structure to quickly get statistics about that table. For example, we can know the number of instances and features with the attribute shape:

```
In : df.shape

Out: (2, 5)
```

We can quickly get the names of the columns with:

```
In : df.columns

Out: Index(['Name', 'Age', 'Profession', 'Nationality',
      'Risk'], dtype='object')
```

Or we could obtain a summary of information about that data frame:

```
In : df.info()

<class 'pandas.core.frame.DataFrame'>
RangeIndex: 2 entries, 0 to 1
Data columns (total 5 columns):
 #   Column       Non-Null Count  Dtype
---  ------       --------------  -----
 0   Name         2 non-null      object
 1   Age          2 non-null      int64
 2   Profession   2 non-null      object
 3   Nationality  2 non-null      object
 4   Risk         2 non-null      bool
dtypes: bool(1), int64(1), object(3)
memory usage: 194.0+ bytes
```

As I said before, each feature of the DataFrame is a Series, which will have a certain data type. For example, the Risk attribute is a boolean True or False, but Name has been classed as object meaning that it could be any data type. If we try to add a new row to a data frame with a different data type on one of the attributes, we may end up changing the data type of the entire series! I will come back to this later.

8.1 Data analysis with the Pandas library

But how do we add a new row to a `DataFrame`. Well, we can simply use the `append` function.

Let me first create a new row (i.e. a `DataFrame` with one row); wait!, I showed you before how to create a `DataFrame` from a dictionary, but you can also call directly the constructor method to create a new `DataFrame`. For that, you need to input the values of each attribute as a list, and indicate the column names like this:

```
In : df2 = pd.DataFrame([["Antonio", 21, "Student",\
                "Spanish", True]],
                columns=['Name', 'Age',\
                        'Profession',\
                        'Nationality',\
                        'Risk'])

In : df2

Out:       Name  Age Profession Nationality  Risk
      0 Antonio   21    Student     Spanish  True
```

We can now append this data frame to the original data frame like this:

```
In : df.append(df2)

Out:        Name  Age Profession Nationality   Risk
      0 Thorsten   45   Lecturer      German   True
      1    Isaac   32   Lecturer     Spanish  False
      0  Antonio   21    Student     Spanish   True
```

Uhm, it seemed to work; we have added `df2` at the bottom of the table, but, don't you spot something weird? The row index for the added row remains at 0... If we don't want this to happen, we have to set a flag `ignore_index` to True, so that, a continuous index value will be maintained.

```
In : df.append(df2, ignore_index= True)

Out:        Name  Age Profession Nationality   Risk
      0 Thorsten   45   Lecturer      German   True
      1    Isaac   32   Lecturer     Spanish  False
      2  Antonio   21    Student     Spanish   True
```

219

8 Getting started with Data Science

Have we modified `df`?

```
In : df

Out:      Name  Age  Profession  Nationality   Risk
       0  Thorsten  45   Lecturer      German   True
       1     Isaac  32   Lecturer     Spanish  False
```

Well, no, the `append` method returns a new object! (hence why it was printed off on the notebook). We should therefore store the result!

```
In : df3 = df.append(df2, ignore_index= True)

In : df3

Out:      Name  Age  Profession  Nationality   Risk
       0  Thorsten  45   Lecturer      German   True
       1     Isaac  32   Lecturer     Spanish  False
       2   Antonio  21    Student     Spanish   True
```

It is important to carefully read the documentation of the Pandas API, so we know how to use it effectively!

Okay, let me try to add the following new row:

```
In : df4 = pd.DataFrame([["Ben", "age", "Student",\
                "German", False]],\
                columns=['Name', 'Age',\
                         'Profession',\
                         'Nationality',\
                         'Risk'])

In : df4

Out:    Name  Age  Profession  Nationality   Risk
     0  Ben  age     Student       German  False
```

Will this work as before?

```
In : df5 = df3.append(df4, ignore_index= True)

In : df5

Out:       Name  Age  Profession  Nationality   Risk
       0  Thorsten  45   Lecturer      German   True
       1     Isaac  32   Lecturer     Spanish  False
       2   Antonio  21    Student     Spanish   True
       3       Ben  age    Student      German  False
```

220

8.1 Data analysis with the Pandas library

Well, maybe unexpectedly, it did work... but shouldn't all data types of a `Series` remain the same? If we check the info of this new data frame:

```
In : df5.info()

<class 'pandas.core.frame.DataFrame'>
RangeIndex: 4 entries, 0 to 3
Data columns (total 5 columns):
 #   Column       Non-Null Count  Dtype
---  ------       --------------  -----
 0   Name         4 non-null      object
 1   Age          4 non-null      object
 2   Profession   4 non-null      object
 3   Nationality  4 non-null      object
 4   Risk         4 non-null      bool
dtypes: bool(1), object(4)
memory usage: 260.0+ bytes
```

We can see that 'Age' is not of `int64` data type any more. Is that a problem? Well, maybe yes.

As I was saying before, Pandas provides a good number of methods that help us obtain quickly statistics about the data. The `describe` method will provide some basic statistics of each numerical feature of the data frame (on the original data frame, only 'age' was numerical):

```
In : df.describe()

Out:              Age
       count   2.000000
       mean   38.500000
       std     9.192388
       min    32.000000
       25%    35.250000
       50%    38.500000
       75%    41.750000
       max    45.000000
```

You can still get some basic statistics for non-numerical features. To do this, we need to explicitly mention the data types of interest in the `include` parameter. Categorical values (i.e. strings) are denoted as type 'object':

221

8 Getting started with Data Science

```
In : df.describe(include=['object'])

Out:          Name  Profession  Nationality
      count    2         2           2
      unique   2         1           2
      top    Isaac    Lecturer    German
      freq     1         2           1
```

For the attribute `risk`, which is not categorical, but a boolean, we can do it like this:

```
In : df.describe(include=['bool'])

Out:         Risk
      count   2
      unique  2
      top   True
      freq    1
```

But if we now apply that on `df5`, the 'Age' attribute will not be treated as numerical `Series`.

```
In : df5.describe()

Out:         Name  Age  Profession  Nationality  Risk
      count   4    4       4            4          4
      unique  4    4       2            2          2
      top    Ben  age   Lecturer     German      True
      freq    1    1       2            2          2
```

So, Pandas is very flexible, but you need to be careful when manipulating it.

Indexing a data frame is similar to the way we access dictionaries. If we want just to get the column with ages:

```
In : df['Age']

Out: 0    45
     1    32
     Name: Age, dtype: int64
```

Can we modify a specific value of a row?

```
In : df5.at[3, 'Age']=32
```

8.1 Data analysis with the Pandas library

```
In : df5

Out:      Name  Age  Profession  Nationality   Risk
     0  Thorsten   45    Lecturer       German   True
     1     Isaac   32    Lecturer      Spanish  False
     2   Antonio   21     Student      Spanish   True
     3       Ben   32     Student       German  False
```

However, if we check the info of `df5`:

```
In : df5.info()

<class 'pandas.core.frame.DataFrame'>
RangeIndex: 4 entries, 0 to 3
Data columns (total 5 columns):
 #   Column       Non-Null Count  Dtype
---  ------       --------------  -----
 0   Name         4 non-null      object
 1   Age          4 non-null      object
 2   Profession   4 non-null      object
 3   Nationality  4 non-null      object
 4   Risk         4 non-null      bool
dtypes: bool(1), object(4)
memory usage: 260.0+ bytes
```

The data type of Age continues to be an object, we can change the data type of a column:

```
In : df5['Age'] = df['Age'].astype('int64')
```

We can also perform operations on a column (remember this is just a `Series`); for example:

```
In : df5['Age'].mean()

Out: 38.5
```

Let me load some more interesting data to run some statistics. Completely anonymised, I have created a table with the marks that students of our Programming course obtained in the different tasks that we use to assess their knowledge. The exam is composed of 4 questions (basics of Python, imperative programming, recursion and OOP). There are also four exercises (Ex01 to Ex04) linked to those topics, and there is a group

8 Getting started with Data Science

project to implement a game with pygame. There are also some additional marks related to on-line quizzes which I have omitted, but they are only a 4% of the final mark.

```
In : results = pd.read_csv('results.csv')
```

We can quickly check some simple statistics about the results:

```
In : results.shape

Out: (61, 10)

In : results.columns

Out: Index(['Question 1', 'Question 2', 'Question 3',
       'Question 4', 'Ex01', 'Ex02',
           'Ex03', 'Ex04', 'Project', 'Total'],
          dtype='object')

In : results.info()

<class 'pandas.core.frame.DataFrame'>
RangeIndex: 61 entries, 0 to 60
Data columns (total 10 columns):
 #   Column       Non-Null Count  Dtype
---  ------       --------------  -----
 0   Question 1   61 non-null     int64
 1   Question 2   61 non-null     int64
 2   Question 3   61 non-null     int64
 3   Question 4   61 non-null     int64
 4   Ex01         61 non-null     int64
 5   Ex02         61 non-null     int64
 6   Ex03         61 non-null     int64
 7   Ex04         61 non-null     int64
 8   Project      61 non-null     int64
 9   Total        61 non-null     int64
dtypes: int64(10)
memory usage: 4.9 KB
```

We can use `describe()` on results to obtain information about all the features at once. Note I am adding `to_latex` to print this nicely for the book.

```
In : results.describe().to_latex
```

8.1 Data analysis with the Pandas library

```
Out: <bound method NDFrame.to_latex of        Question 1
     Question 2    Question 3    Question
     4         Ex01           Ex02    \
     count    61.000000    61.000000    61.000000    61.000000
     61.000000    61.000000
     mean     18.770492    15.622951    11.016393    13.327869
     91.311475    86.147541
     std       5.556958     5.342172     7.603709     8.096751
     11.686946    10.303456
     min       3.000000     4.000000     0.000000     0.000000
     60.000000    60.000000
     25%      17.000000    11.000000     4.000000     6.000000
     90.000000    80.000000
     50%      20.000000    17.000000    12.000000    14.000000
     95.000000    85.000000
     75%      23.000000    20.000000    17.000000    21.000000
     100.000000   90.000000
     max      25.000000    25.000000    25.000000    25.000000
     100.000000   100.000000

                    Ex03          Ex04      Project       Total
     count    61.000000    61.000000    61.000000    61.000000
     mean     81.721311    73.688525    76.606557    69.032787
     std      12.345217    22.856466    14.689314    14.490189
     min      45.000000     0.000000     0.000000    26.000000
     25%      75.000000    60.000000    70.000000    62.000000
     50%      80.000000    80.000000    75.000000    70.000000
     75%      90.000000    90.000000    85.000000    80.000000
     max     100.000000   100.000000   100.000000    94.000000   >
```

We can see that the questions of the exams are marked up to 25 marks each, but the exercises, the project and the total are evaluated out of 100. We are going to learn how to visualise the data later, but I would like to play a bit with this data frame. Let's sort the table by the final mark in descending order:

```
In : results.sort_values(by='Total', ascending=False)\
     .head().to_latex

Out: <bound method NDFrame.to_latex of        Question 1
     Question 2    Question 3    Question 4
     Ex01    Ex02    Ex03    Ex04    \
     6                     21              25         20          24
     95      85      100     100
     36                    25              17         24          23
     100     90      80      100
```

225

8 Getting started with Data Science

```
    48              25              21        16           25
   100      90      95     100
    14              19              22        14           25
    95      90      65      80
    26              20              19        21           24
    75      90      75      70

         Project  Total
    6      100     94
   36       95     92
   48       90     90
   14       97     86
   26       93     86   >
```

How many people got less than 50 marks on Exercise 04?

```
In  : results[results['Ex04']<50].count()

Out: Question 1    8
     Question 2    8
     Question 3    8
     Question 4    8
     Ex01          8
     Ex02          8
     Ex03          8
     Ex04          8
     Project       8
     Total         8
     dtype: int64
```

Interesting, so we can index a data frame and create a new one by using a logical condition (similar to functional programming). This is called boolean indexing and it is very convenient. Basically, you just need to include some logical condition that is going to be checked for each element of the Name column. The result of this kind of indexing is a new data frame that consists only of those rows that satisfy the condition on that column.

How many of them got a mark between 50 and 60?

```
In  : results[(results['Ex04']>=50) &\
              (results['Ex04']<60)].count()

Out: Question 1    6
     Question 2    6
```

8.1 Data analysis with the Pandas library

```
Question 3    6
Question 4    6
Ex01          6
Ex02          6
Ex03          6
Ex04          6
Project       6
Total         6
dtype: int64
```

Challenge 1: Select the three students with the highest mark in 'Ex04', and show only the first 4 columns of the data frame (Question 1 to Question 4). **Hint**: you may want to look at the `iloc()` function to index the data frame by number (Section 8.5.1)

Using a functional programming style, we can apply functions to columns of our data frame using the function `apply`.

```
In : results[results['Ex04'].apply(lambda mark:\
                                   mark <50)].count()
```

```
Out: Question 1    8
     Question 2    8
     Question 3    8
     Question 4    8
     Ex01          8
     Ex02          8
     Ex03          8
     Ex04          8
     Project       8
     Total         8
     dtype: int64
```

I would now like to have an additional column to the data frame that rather than having the numerical 'Total' mark, it would have the final classification (e.g. Fail <50, Pass [50,60) , merit [60,70) or distinction >=70). How do we do this?

```
In : def degreeClassification(n):
         if n < 50:
             return 'Fail'
         elif n<60:
             return 'Pass'
         elif n<70:
             return 'Merit'
```

8 Getting started with Data Science

```
        else:
            return 'Distinction'

    results['Classification'] =\
        results['Total'].map(
            lambda n:degreeClassification(n))
    results.head().to_latex
```

```
Out: <bound method NDFrame.to_latex of        Question 1
     Question 2   Question 3   Question 4
     Ex01    Ex02    Ex03    Ex04   \
     0               18              16              23              22      100
     85      80      70
     1               20              13              11              22      100
     85      80      90
     2               7               7               0               2       100
     100     85      30
     3               14              16              4               13      95
     95      100     55
     4               4               6               0               0       65
     95      65      25

            Project   Total  Classification
     0           80      81      Distinction
     1           93      79      Distinction
     2           70      42             Fail
     3           87      67            Merit
     4           70      39             Fail  >
```

So, to create a new column, we simply need to 'index' a column with a new name (above 'Classification'), then we used a map function to convert the numerical values into degree classifications.

8.2 Visualising your data

When analysing data, Pandas is frequently coupled together with the *Matplotlib* and the *seaborn* libraries to visualise tabular data. You can install these two libraries very easily with `pip install matplotlib`. Here I will show you just a few examples of what you can do with these two libraries and Pandas.

228

8.2 Visualising your data

```
In : import matplotlib.pyplot as plt
     import seaborn as sns
     sns.set()
```

We can easily plot a histogram of a specific attribute:

```
In : results['Total'].hist()
Out: <matplotlib.axes._subplots.AxesSubplot at 0x11040a400>
```

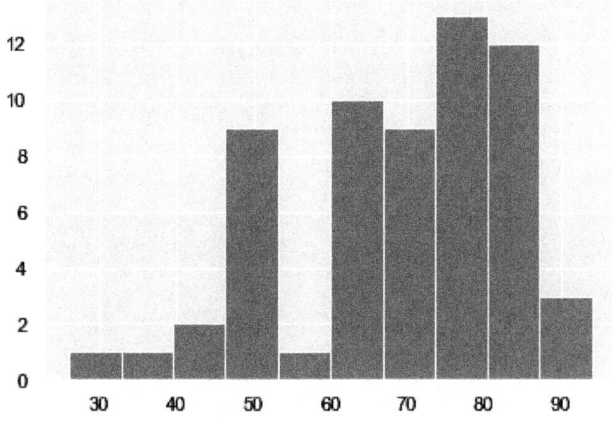

On the above plot we see the number of students in the different intervals according to their final `Total` mark.
But if you prefer density plots:

```
In : results['Total'].plot(kind='density', figsize=(12, 4));
```

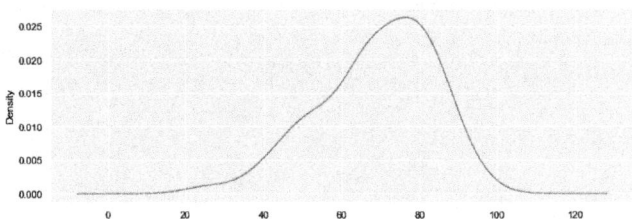

229

8 Getting started with Data Science

When using plot, we have set a number of options, such as the kind of plot (indicating 'density'), and the size of the figure. There are many more options that you can explore!

With sns, we can also plot a distribution of observations:

```
In : sns.distplot(results['Total']);
```

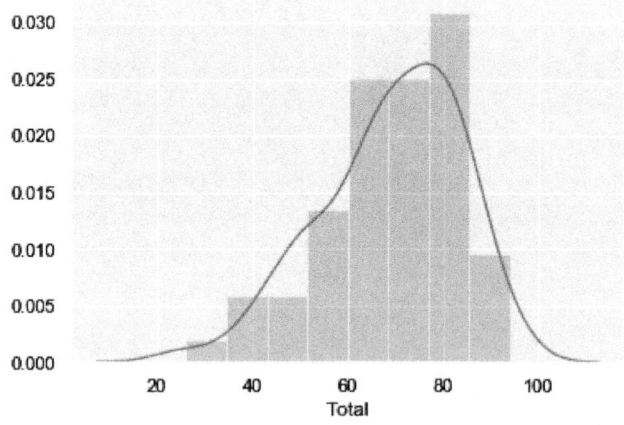

We can also do create a heatmap by simply doing this:

```
In : corr_matrix = results.corr()
     sns.heatmap(corr_matrix);
```

8.3 Mining the data

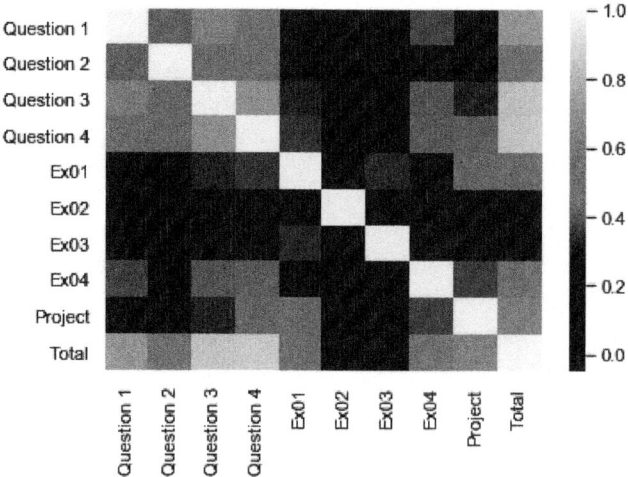

I was interested in seeing whether there is any correlation between the marks obtained in the different assessments and the total or not. The above heatmap helps us see the correlation between all the attributes!

It seems quite interesting to see that there is a high correlation between the marks of question 4 and the total mark!

8.3 Mining the data

8.3.1 A regression approach

One thing I would like to know as a lecturer is how well my students will perform in the exam after assessing their exercises. So the question I would like to answer is... could I predict the total mark of a student based on their exercise marks? Looking at the previous correlation matrix, well, none of the exercise marks seemed to be very correlated. But, let's see if we can do something with this.

8 Getting started with Data Science

We are going to try to answer that question by using a supervised regression approach. In data mining, regression[4] is a kind of supervised learning, which aims to learn a function that maps a number of input variables with a target output (which is a real number). It is called supervised learning because we assume that we have some initial data from which we can learn that mapping between the variables. In our case, we have the data from 61 students, and what we want to learn is what's the relation between exercise marks (including their project mark) and the total mark the students obtained.

Let's first prepare our data in the correct shape. I want to keep a data frame X with the marks of Ex01 to Ex04, and the project. And what I would like to be able to predict is, given X, what's going to be the 'Total' mark. So, I am going to store the target output in a different data frame y. Just like this:

```
In : X = results.loc[:,'Ex01':'Project']
     y = results['Total']
```

I have used slicing here with the `loc` function to select all the rows and the columns from Ex01 to Project.

Okay, so in data mining and machine learning, it is important that we used our data sensibly. And that means that we need to make sure that if we learn such a mapping function, we need to be able to test that this works on unseen data. There are different validation approaches for machine learning, but here we are going to simply split the data into a training partition containing 70% of the data, and the remaining data will be used to check whether we have learned correctly the mapping or not.

As mentioned at the beginning of the book, we are using the scikit-learn library[5] to apply different machine learning and data mining methods. And this library comes with a good number of tools to manipulate data frames. So we can split the data (randomly) using the following function:

```
In : from sklearn.model_selection import train_test_split
```

---
[4]https://en.wikipedia.org/wiki/Regression_analysis
[5]https://scikit-learn.org/stable/

8.3 Mining the data

```
In : X_train,X_test,y_train,y_test = \
        train_test_split(X,y,\
                    test_size=0.3,\
                    random_state=1)
```

The names of the variables for training or test, input and output are entirely up to you. However, we typically use capital X to refer to the input matrices, and y to refer the class label vectors.

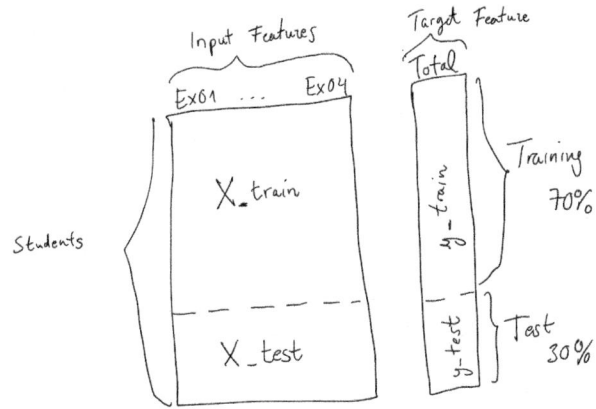

```
In : y_train.count()
```

Out: 42

```
In : y_test.count()
```

Out: 19

So now, we have 4 different data frames. What we are assuming here is that we are learning the mapping between X_train and y_train. Then, when we have achieved that (I'll show you a few techniques to do this), we will want to see whether we are able to predict the Total mark for a set of students we haven't used for training. For those students, X_test, we only know the marks on the exercises, and we will try to infer the total mark. Then, we will compare the prediction with the actual mark (available on y_test).

233

Alright, so now we need to do the mapping. There are many different supervised learning algorithms, and each algorithm will have its strengths and weaknesses. There isn't such a thing like the best algorithm. The scikit-learn library provides the most relevant algorithms, including Linear Regression, Nearest Neighbours, Support Vector Machines, or Decision Trees. I am not going to detail how all of these algorithms work, but I am going to show you how to use the scikit-learn library from a few of them. If you want to know more, you should look at the details of the scikit-learn API.

However, to give you a flavour of how this kind of algorithms work, I will briefly explain how one of the simplest machine learning algorithm, the k-Nearest neighbour algorithm[6], works. This algorithm is all about computing the similarity between examples. So if we want to predict the mark of a new student based on the exercise marks, well, let's find who are the k students in the training data with the most similar exercise marks. This is typically done by computing the Euclidean distance between the input instance (e.g. student X, with marks 60, 80, 80, 87 and 90, respectively) and the entire training data (i.e. `X_train`).

Scikit learn has a package `neighbors` that we import like this:

In : **from sklearn import** neighbors

We are doing regression, so we will use the `KNeighborsRegressor` class. It may have multiple parameters, but we are only going to set the number of neighbours that will be considered when computing distances (e.g. 3).

We initialise the algorithm like this:

In : regr = neighbors.KNeighborsRegressor(3)

Then, we are ready to 'fit' the data (i.e. create that mapping). Funnily enough, the Nearest Neighbour algorithm doesn't really do anything in this stage (as this is a lazy learning algorithm), but the scikit-learn library kept this function to unify

---

[6]https://en.wikipedia.org/wiki/K-nearest_neighbors_algorithm

8.3 Mining the data

the way all machine learning methods work in their library. The input for this stage is the training data:

```
In : regr.fit(X_train, y_train)

Out: KNeighborsRegressor(algorithm='auto', leaf_size=30,
    metric='minkowski',
            metric_params=None, n_jobs=1,
    n_neighbors=3, p=2,
            weights='uniform')
```

We are now in a good position to predict the marks for those students we did use for training (`X_test`).

```
In : y_pred= regr.predict(X_test)

In : print(y_pred.tolist())

[57.0, 77.0, 70.0, 70.33333333333333, 64.0,
78.66666666666667, 69.66666666666667,
84.66666666666667, 70.0, 79.33333333333333,
59.333333333333336, 75.0, 77.33333333333333,
69.66666666666667, 80.33333333333333, 74.0, 63.0, 54.0,
79.0]


In : print(y_test.values)

[48 66 42 52 52 86 73 92 47 85 65 83 67 67 83 74 64 50
75]
```

So, you can see that the algorithm predicted some values for each student, but how good was that prediction? In data mining, we typically use error measures (or accuracy measures) to determine the success of the prediction. In regression, a very common error measure is the mean absolute error that as the name indicate computes the mean absolute error in the prediction of all test students. Once again, the scikit-learn library has implemented multiple functions to do this for you:

```
In : from sklearn.metrics import mean_absolute_error

    mean_absolute_error(y_test,y_pred)
```

8 Getting started with Data Science

```
Out: 8.596491228070175
```

This is telling us that we can predict the total mark a student with a 8.59 error in the marks, which is not particularly great, but not too bad either. Shall we try other regression models to see if they are more precise?

Linear regression[7] is probably something you've heard about before; this consists of minimising a cost function that aims to determine the best coefficients that multiply each feature value to obtain the target value. To run this model on scikit-learn, we simply have to import the package `linear_model` and follow the exact same pipeline as before:

```
In : from sklearn import linear_model

    regr = linear_model.LinearRegression()
    regr.fit(X_train, y_train)
    y_pred = regr.predict(X_test)

    mean_absolute_error(y_test,y_pred)

Out: 9.444895205936287
```

In this case, it turns out to be slightly worse than the nearest neighbour algorithm, but if you run the `train_test_split` function with a different `random_state`, you may get a different result as the partitioning into training/test is random.

We can also run other classical machine learning algorithms. For example, I very much like Decision Trees[8], which partition the data into different subsets depending on the input attributes. The aim is to create a (mapping) model that predicts the target value by learning decision rules inferred from the data features.

```
In : from sklearn.tree import DecisionTreeRegressor

    regr = DecisionTreeRegressor(random_state=0,\
                        max_depth=2)
```

---

[7]https://scikit-learn.org/stable/modules/linear_model.html
[8]https://scikit-learn.org/stable/modules/tree.html

8.3 Mining the data

```
regr.fit(X_train, y_train)
y_pred=regr.predict(X_test)

mean_absolute_error(y_test,y_pred)
```
Out: 12.243567251461988

In this particular example (and with the parameters I used), well, it doesn't perform better than the previous methods, but what I like from Decision Trees is that you can visualise how the method actually works (the decision rules that have been inferred). You can visualise the 'tree', using the following code. But first, make sure you have installed the `pydotplus` library.

```
In : from ipywidgets import Image
     from io import StringIO
     import pydotplus
     from sklearn.tree import export_graphviz
     dot_data = StringIO()
     export_graphviz(regr, feature_names=X_train.columns,\
                     out_file=dot_data, filled=True)
     graph = pydotplus.graph_from_dot_data\
             (dot_data.getvalue())
     graph.write_png("regression.png")
```
Out: True

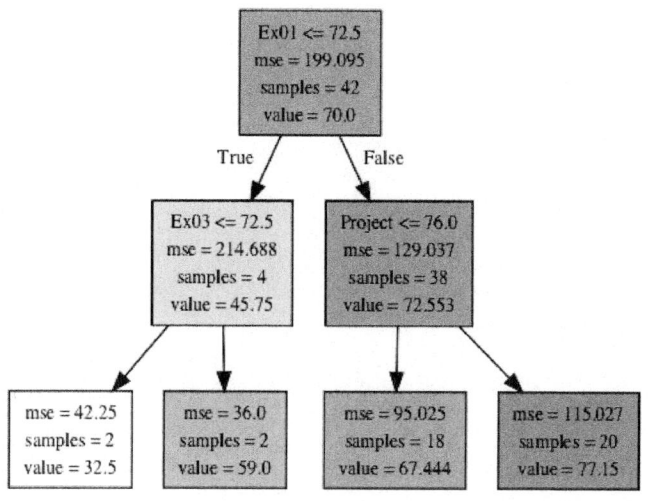

237

The tree is so 'small' (only two levels) because I intentionally used the parameter `max_depth=2` when creating the Decision Tree. You may want to play with that parameter to see if the result changes!

We can interpret this tree as follows:

- If the mark of Ex01 is less or equal than 72.5 and the Ex03 mark is less or equal than 72.5, the final mark is 32.5.
- If the mark of Ex01 is less or equal than 72.5 and the project mark is more than 72.5, the final mark is 59.
- If the mark of Ex01 is greater than 72.5 and the Project mark is less or equal than 76, the final mark is 67.44.
- If the mark of Ex01 is greater than 72.5 and the Project mark is greater than 76, the final mark is 77.15.

These are very simple rules that have been inferred from the data, and of course, it is not working really well in this case. But this kind of algorithm offers this additional interpretability that is becoming a hot topic in Artificial Intelligence (why the machine decided to do that?).

Another classical method which is typically very robust is Random Forests[9]. This method is actually based on decision trees, but rather than learning a single tree from the data, it learns multiple tree for different feature subsets (i.e. it doesn't use all the feature at once). Let's run it:

```
In : from sklearn.ensemble import RandomForestRegressor

    clf = RandomForestRegressor(max_depth=5,\
                random_state=1, n_estimators=100)
    clf = clf.fit(X_train, y_train)
    y_pred=clf.predict(X_test)

    mean_absolute_error(y_test,y_pred)

Out: 8.629096280164626
```

Funnily enough, the k-nearest neighbour algorithm continues to be the best algorithm in this case. As said before, there

---

[9] https://scikit-learn.org/stable/modules/ensemble.html

8.3 Mining the data

are many other methods, and I encourage you to test different algorithms understanding their way of working!

Challenge 2: I haven't told you how we weighted the different exercises (Ex01 to Ex04), project mark, and exam questions (Q1 to Q2) to compute the total mark. Could you apply any of the previous methods to approximately compute the weights of each part?

Hint: Some models will provide you the feature_importance or coefficients after learning (Section 8.5.2)

8.3.2 A classification approach

Rather than aiming to predict the actual mark, could we try to predict the final classification (i.e. pass, fail, etc)? If we embark ourselves in such a task (you might think it is easier, but not necessarily), we are going to be doing supervised classification. In data mining, classification[10] also aims to learn that mapping between input variables and an output variable, but in this case, the target output is not a number, but a categorical value (we normally call **'class label'**). So, we will aim to see if the exercise marks help us to predict the total mark 'category' that the students will belong. In our case, we have four different categories (Fail, Pass, Merit and Distinction); this is known as multi-class classification[11]!

Once again, we start off by preparing the data. The input variables are exactly the same as before, but the target output will be the Classification column.

```
In : Xc = results.loc[:,'Ex01':'Project']
     yc = results['Classification']
```

Let's split the data as before:

```
In : Xc_train,Xc_test,yc_train,yc_test =\
        train_test_split(Xc,yc,\
                         test_size=0.3,\
                         random_state=6)
```

---
[10]https://en.wikipedia.org/wiki/Statistical_classification
[11]https://en.wikipedia.org/wiki/Multiclass_classification

8 Getting started with Data Science

If we now want to apply some machine learning algorithms from the scikit-learning library, we only need to make sure we use a 'classifier' (and not a regression algorithm). Most of the algorithms we used before, can also be used as classifiers. Let's try with the k nearest neighbours algorithm. This will follow the exact same pipeline as before:

```
In : clf = neighbors.KNeighborsClassifier(3)
     clf = clf.fit(Xc_train, yc_train)
     yc_pred= clf.predict(Xc_test)
```

However, how do we now measure the error in classifying those students?

```
In : yc_pred

Out: array(['Distinction', 'Merit', 'Distinction',
       'Distinction',
            'Distinction', 'Distinction', 'Distinction',
       'Pass', 'Merit',
            'Distinction', 'Distinction', 'Distinction',
       'Distinction',
            'Distinction', 'Distinction', 'Distinction',
       'Distinction',
            'Distinction', 'Distinction'], dtype=object)
```

Something I didn't mention before is that the prediction returned by scikit-learn (i.e. `yc_pred`) is of a certain data type we haven't seen before.

```
In : type(yc_pred)

Out: numpy.ndarray
```

Numpy[12] is a very well-known Python library that allows us to work with arrays (rather than lists!). If we now want to know the length of that array, we need to use the attribute `size`:

```
In : yc_pred.size

Out: 19
```

---
[12] https://www.numpy.org/

8.3 Mining the data

```
In : yc_test

Out: 32    Distinction
     7     Distinction
     0     Distinction
     59    Distinction
     34    Distinction
     23           Pass
     39    Distinction
     21          Merit
     50    Distinction
     43           Fail
     3           Merit
     40           Fail
     48    Distinction
     60          Merit
     6     Distinction
     30    Distinction
     53    Distinction
     14    Distinction
     24          Merit
Name: Classification, dtype: object
```

Uhm, we can't use the mean absolute error, because we cannot compute the differences between a prediction and the real category in the same way. In classification, the most used performance measure is accuracy; this measures how many times a classifier has hit the right prediction relative to the total number of classifications. We can use this measure like this:

```
In : from sklearn.metrics import accuracy_score

In : accuracy_score(yc_test,yc_pred)

Out: 0.5263157894736842
```

This is not very promising. This means that only 52.63% of the times (10 out of 19) we are able to predict the right final degree classification :-(

Another way to understand better the performance of a method is to look at the Confusion Matrix[13]. This error matrix presents in each row the instances in a predicted class, while each column represents the instance in an actual class (or viceversa). Scikit-learn provides this kind of confusion matrix:

---

[13]https://en.wikipedia.org/wiki/Confusion_matrix

8 Getting started with Data Science

```
In : from sklearn.metrics import confusion_matrix
     confusion_matrix(yc_test, yc_pred, \
                     labels=["Distinction",\
                             "Merit", "Pass",\
                             "Fail"], sample_weight=None)

Out: array([[10,  2,  0,  0],
            [ 3,  0,  1,  0],
            [ 1,  0,  0,  0],
            [ 2,  0,  0,  0]])
```

How do we read this? The first row and column represent the class 'Distinction'; second row and column represent 'Merit', and so on. Rows represent the actual classes, and columns the predictions.

If we look at the diagonal of that matrix, we can know when the actual target values and the predicted values were the same. So, we can see that 10 times, the predicted class was `Distinction`, and it was right. However, the classifier did never get correctly the examples from the rest of the classes. Interestingly, the classifier never predicted an example from class `Fail`(see last column).

Why is this problem being so difficult? When I deal with a classification problem, I'm always interested in the class distribution, which is the number of examples/instances that we have for each class label. Let's compute that for each class:

```
In : yc_train[yc_train=='Distinction'].count()

Out: 21

In : yc_train[yc_train=='Merit'].count()

Out: 10

In : yc_train[yc_train=='Pass'].count()

Out: 7

In : yc_train[yc_train=='Fail'].count()

Out: 4
```

8.3 Mining the data

Interestingly, the distribution of classes seems to be very imbalanced. In this case, using accuracy might not be the best choice to measure the performance of a classifier (i.e. classifying everything as Distinction would provide a higher accuracy rate, 12 out of 19 - roughly 63%). Thus, we should focus on the confusion matrix to understand if we can classify correctly the students,

Okay, why don't we try another classifier? For example a Decision Tree:

```
In : from sklearn.tree import DecisionTreeClassifier

    clf = DecisionTreeClassifier(random_state=0,\
                                 max_depth=2)
    clf.fit(Xc_train, yc_train)
    yc_pred=clf.predict(Xc_test)

    accuracy_score(yc_test,yc_pred)
Out: 0.631578947368421

In : confusion_matrix(yc_test, yc_pred, \
                    labels=["Distinction", "Merit",\
                    "Pass", "Fail"],\
                    sample_weight=None)
Out: array([[10, 2, 0, 0],
            [ 2, 2, 0, 0],
            [ 0, 1, 0, 0],
            [ 0, 2, 0, 0]])
```

Well, this one provided a better result, as it is able to predict correctly two merits!

Let's have a look at the tree:

```
In : from ipywidgets import Image
    from io import StringIO
    import pydotplus
    from sklearn.tree import export_graphviz
    dot_data = StringIO()
    export_graphviz(clf, feature_names=Xc_train.columns,\
                    out_file=dot_data, filled=True)
    graph = pydotplus.graph_from_dot_data\
            (dot_data.getvalue())
    graph.write_png("classification.png")
```

243

8 Getting started with Data Science

```
Out: True
```

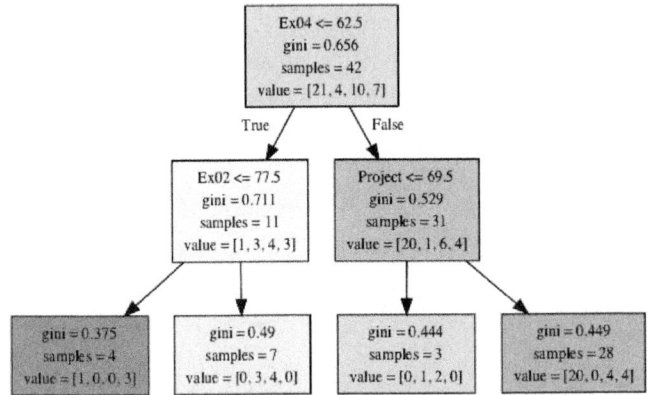

Let's transcribe this into rules. To interpret correctly this tree, we need to understand the meaning of that 'value=[list of number]" that is provided within each node. This provides the number of instances/examples of each class label in the node. But it doesn't tell you to which class each position of the list. To figure that out, we can check how the Decision Tree defined the classes:

```
In : clf.classes_

Out: array(['Distinction', 'Fail', 'Merit', 'Pass'],
     dtype=object)
```

So, Position 0 in that list is Distinction, position 1 - Fail, 2 - Merit, 3 is Pass.

Each leaf node of the tree will be labelled with the class with more examples.

- If the mark of Ex04 is less or equal than 62.5 and the mark of Ex02 is less or equal than 77.5, the degree classification is 'Pass'.
- If the mark of Ex04 is less or equal than 62.5 and the mark of Ex02 is greater than 77.5, the degree classification is 'Merit'.

- If the mark of Ex04 is greater than 62.5 and the mark of Ex04 is less or equal than 69.5, the degree classification is 'Merit'.
- If the mark of Ex04 is greater than 62.5 and the mark of Ex04 is greater than 69.5, the degree classification is 'Distinction'.

Aren't these rules weird? There is no rule that tells you when to classify something as a `Fail`!.

Challenge 3: How would you train the Decision Tree to obtain more sensible rules? So that we can classify students of all categories!

Suggested approaches: You can either (1) play with the parameters of the Decision Tree classifier; (2) the class distribution is imbalanced, so you may want to modify the training partition to keep a balanced distribution before training the model (Section 8.5.3)

8.4 Summary

We can easily apply data science approaches with Python and the programming concepts you have learned in this book. Below I summarise a few take-home messages from this chapter:

- In machine learning, we are frequently provided with tabular data consisting of a number of examples/instances with a given number of features. Typically, instances are represented as rows, and features as columns of a matrix. The values of some of these features are known in advance (input features), but there might be feature(s) for which we would like to know/predict their value automatically. For example, we may be provided with information about potential cancer patients for which we know a number of (input) features/Attributes (e.g. age, gender, smokers, blood tests, etc), and we would like to know whether they have cancer or not (the output feature).

- One of the most common goals in machine learning is to predict the value of one (or more) of those features for a new unseen example/instance. We call that feature(s), the target output(s). Depending on the nature of the target output, we talk about different machine learning approaches. Real-value outputs are addressed with **regression algorithms**, while categorical outputs are dealt with **classification approaches**.

- To do this, supervised classification and regression approaches aim to learn (or establish) a mapping between input features and the target output(s), using some training data ('limited' amount of data that has been annotated in advance). There is a wide variety of approaches, and they all have different advantages and disadvantages. There isn't such a thing as the best machine learning algorithm (although there are some approaches that highlight by the robustness in many problems, for example, deep learning approaches are becoming very popular).

- There are many other machine learning areas that have not been covered or even mentioned in this book (e.g. unsupervised learning, semi-supervised learning), as our objective was to simply show a few examples of how to get started with data science with the programming concepts you have learned so far.

- The Pandas library offers a data structure called Data Frame that allows us to use manipulate tabular data very easily and obtain statistics. In conjunction with other libraries such as MatPlotLib and seaborn, we can get fancy plots to represent our data.

- The scikit-learn library provides a great number of machine learning and data mining techniques that work on Data Frames. Additional packages area also provided to perform appropriate validation and measure the error or success of the predictions.

8.5 Solutions to Challenges

8.5.1 Challenge 1

Select the three students with the highest mark in 'Ex04', and show only the first 4 columns of the data frame (Question 1 to Question 4). **Hint**: you may want to look at the iloc() to index the data frame by number.

```
In : results.sort_values(by='Ex04',\
                    ascending=False).iloc[0:3,0:4]

Out:      Question 1   Question 2   Question 3   Question 4
   21          21           17            6           20
   36          25           17           24           23
    6          21           25           20           24
```

8.5.2 Challenge 2

I haven't told you how we weighted the different exercises (Ex01 to Ex04), project mark, and exam questions (Q1 to Q2) to compute the total mark. Could you apply any of the previous methods to compute the weights of each part?

Hint: Some models will provide you the feature_importance or coefficients after learning .

So, first we create the dataset from the original data frame. In this case the input features will be all the exercises, exam questions and the project mark. The output will be the 'Total' mark.

```
In : X = results.loc[:,'Question 1':'Project']
     y = results['Total']
```

What we want to do is to learn the mapping between X and y, and print the weights. As we are not aiming to predict anything, just learning the mapping, we could feed X and y as the input parameters of a machine learning algorithm to learn the mapping. In particular, a very simple linear regression would do the job:

8 Getting started with Data Science

```
In : from sklearn import linear_model

    regr = linear_model.LinearRegression()
    regr.fit(X, y)

Out: LinearRegression(copy_X=True, fit_intercept=True,
    n_jobs=1, normalize=False)
```

We can check how well the model fit the data:

```
In : regr.score(X, y)

Out: 0.9943956817950749
```

And now, just simple check the coefficients that have been computed:

```
In : regr.coef_

Out: array([0.54661248, 0.44966587, 0.52490231, 0.47629255,
    0.05742466,
        0.02052757, 0.04366407, 0.05008801, 0.31955185])
```

Are they any good??

Well, the exam counted as 50% of the final mark (each question counted equally). Hence why you see that most numbers are around 0.5 (note that the mark is out of 25 for each exam question!

The exercises were roughly 16% of the final mark (so each question contributed roughly a 4%).

The project was valued a 30% of the final mark), and the remaining 4% comes from quizzes. As I haven't provided the quiz marks, the numbers are not perfect (neither the correlation), but it gives you a good approximation as to how we did it.

8.5.3 Challenge 3

How would you train the Decision Tree to obtain more sensible rules? So that we can classify students of all categories!

Suggested approaches: You can either (1) play with the parameters of the Decision Tree classifier; (2) the class distribution

8.5 Solutions to Challenges

is imbalanced, so you may want to modify the training partition to keep a balanced distribution before training the model

The easiest thing to do is to make the decision tree aware that the class distribution is a bit imbalanced, and therefore. You can do that by modifying the parameter `class_weight`. You could do it manually (indicating the weight for each class), or we can also tell it to 'balance' it.

```
In : clf = DecisionTreeClassifier(random_state=0,\
                                  max_depth=2,\
                                  class_weight="balanced")
     clf.fit(Xc_train, yc_train)
     yc_pred=clf.predict(Xc_test)

     accuracy_score(yc_test,yc_pred)

Out: 0.6842105263157895

In : confusion_matrix(yc_test,\
                     yc_pred, labels=["Distinction",\
                                      "Merit", "Pass",\
                                      "Fail"])

Out: array([[10,  1,  0,  1],
            [ 3,  1,  0,  0],
            [ 0,  1,  0,  0],
            [ 0,  0,  0,  2]])
```

We haven't predicted well any example of the class `Pass`. But let's look at the tree to see if that makes more sense than before.

```
In : from ipywidgets import Image
     from io import StringIO
     import pydotplus
     from sklearn.tree import export_graphviz
     dot_data = StringIO()
     export_graphviz(clf, feature_names=Xc_train.columns,\
                     out_file=dot_data, filled=True)
     graph = pydotplus.graph_from_dot_data\
             (dot_data.getvalue())
     graph.write_png("classificationBalanced.png")

Out: True
```

249

8 Getting started with Data Science

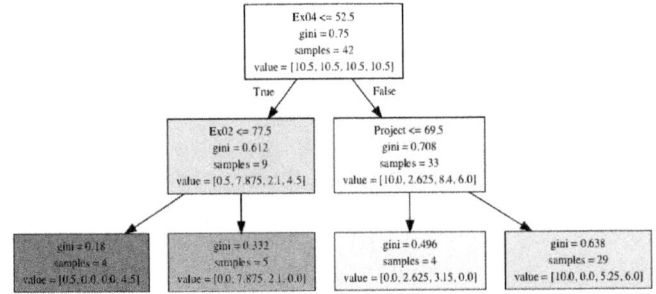

```
In : clf.classes_

Out: array(['Distinction', 'Fail', 'Merit', 'Pass'],
     dtype=object)
```

So, Position 0 in that list is Distinction, position 1 - Fail, 2 - Merit, 3 is Pass.

Each leaf node of the tree will be labelled with the class with more examples.

- If the mark of Ex04 is less or equal than 52.5 and the mark of Ex02 is less or equal than 77.5, the degree classification is 'Pass'.
- If the mark of Ex04 is less or equal than 52.5 and the mark of Ex02 is greater than 77.5, the degree classification is 'Fail'.
- If the mark of Ex04 is greater than 52.5 and the Project mark is less or equal than 69.5, the degree classification is 'Merit'.
- If the mark of Ex04 is greater than 52.5 and the Project mark is greater than 69.5, the degree classification is 'Distinction'.

This time the rules make more sense than before, and the algorithm has created a model that could classify a student in the four categories. The accuracy of 68% is not extremely high but you could maybe try to see if there are outliers or other ways to improve the method with this data.

250

8.6 Exercises

We want to use a data science approach to learn how to play the Pong game we implemented in the previous chapter. We can certainly do this without any machine learning, but this is way more fun, and also it will learn to play the way that you do it. The following steps should help you achieve this:

1- **Gathering the data**: modify the latest version of the game to log how the user moves the paddle (paddle.y) with respect to the position and speed of the ball.

Hint: you should print the values every iteration of the loop on a file (i.e. `open("gameData.csv", 'w')` and investigate how to use the `print` function to output everything on that file).

Whenever you have done this, you should play the game for a little while, and create a file. It is important to play the game for a bit to gather enough data.

Then, you can read the file you just generated:

```
In : pong = pd.read_csv('gameData-new.csv')
```

This is how my file looks like:

```
In : pong.head()
```

```
Out:      x    y   vx  vy  paddle.y
     0  770  200  -4  -4       200
     1  770  200  -4  -4       314
     2  770  200  -4  -4       314
     3  770  200  -4  -4       314
     4  770  200  -4  -4       314
```

```
In : pong.describe()
```

```
Out:                    x                y              vx
       vy        paddle.y
       count  15635.000000     15635.000000     15635.000000
       15635.000000   15635.000000
       mean     411.807227       199.711417        -0.148129
       0.005373     197.372114
       std      219.384330        97.700268         3.997384
       4.000124      33.690472
       min       30.000000        32.000000        -4.000000
```

251

8 Getting started with Data Science

```
       -4.000000    60.000000
25%   222.000000   116.000000   -4.000000
       -4.000000   193.000000
50%   414.000000   200.000000   -4.000000
        4.000000   198.000000
75%   606.000000   284.000000    4.000000
        4.000000   202.000000
max   770.000000   368.000000    4.000000
        4.000000   340.000000

In : pong['x'].count()

Out: 15635
```

As you can see, I have created a log file of more than 15 thousand moves that we are going to use to learn.

Hint: Before doing any learning, maybe you should consider removing duplicates from the data

2- Using this data, the goal is to predict the position of the paddle (so the target output is `paddle.y`) with respect to the position of the Ball (input features). So, you should create training and test partitions and try a number of Regression algorithms (e.g. RandomForest, k-NN). Measure the error in predicting the position of the paddle, and select the most accurate model.

Hint: after deciding which regression method works better, I would retrain the model with all the data!

3- Incorporate the prediction model to control the position of the paddle automatically. Thus, you have a game that plays itself!

Hint: You may want to change the update method of the Paddle class to control the position of the paddle with the predicted value rather than using the mouse position.

4- To make the game a bit more interesting, add a second Paddle on the left of the screen that will be manually control, so you can now play against the model you learn before.

Printed in Great Britain
by Amazon